SCOTT TINLEY'S WINNING TRIATHLON

SCOTT TINLEY'S WINNING TRIATHLON

BY SCOTT TINLEY WITH MIKE PLANT

CONTEMPORARY
BOOKS, INC.
CHICAGO

Library of Congress Cataloging-in-Publication Data

Tinley, Scott.
    Scott Tinley's Winning triathlon.

    Includes index.
    1. Triathlon.   2. Triathlon—Training.
3. Triathlon—Psychological aspects.   I. Plant, Mike.
II. Title.   III. Title: Winning triathlon.
GV1060.7.T56   1986   796.4'07   85-30911
ISBN 0-8092-5117-5

Published by Contemporary Books, Inc.
180 North Michigan Avenue, Chicago, Illinois 60601
Manufactured in the United States of America
Library of Congress Catalog Card Number: 85-30911
International Standard Book Number: 0-8092-5117-5

Published simultaneously in Canada by Beaverbooks, Ltd.
195 Allstate Parkway, Valleywood Business Park
Markham, Ontario L3R 4T8 Canada

All photographs by Mike Plant unless otherwise credited.

CONTENTS

To all my competitors, especially The Man, The Grip, and the Terminator. Thanks for pushing me to my limit, pushing back the barriers. You guys are great—but I'm gonna get you!

FOREWORD

In the early 1980s, when I was beginning to think seriously about doing a marathon, I grew concerned about being able to run the miles I needed without breaking down. I wasn't a kid anymore, and I knew that as a runner moves into his thirties his ability to recover from racing and training decreases.

I'd already learned the value of supplemental exercise. I'd always been active in watersports and I'd been training with weights for several years. Running is great, I love it, but it's good for only one thing: running. Basically a runner is in shape for running and that's about all.

I began to look at how athletes in other sports handled recovery during heavy training, and at triathletes in particular. They seemed to be the experts. Dave Scott and Scott Tinley, of course, were right at the top of the list. I was amazed at what they could do. Here I was worrying about running twenty-six miles and these guys were doing it after swimming for an hour and bicycling for 112 miles. "If they can do *that*," I thought to myself . . .

I followed Scott Tinley's career casually, and he became my favorite. We seemed a lot alike somehow, and when I finally met him at a trade show, he was just as I had imagined: laid back and casual, but very confident. He races that way, too. The expression on his face when he competes is tough and determined, and you can tell he is racing from the heart, because he loves it. On the other hand, I never felt that he's an athlete who is totally obsessed. You get the impression at the end of every competition that he's got a little bit left, that he's saved something for the party that night.

Scott Tinley's greatest success has been his ability to perform consistently over the years. He placed third in the Ironman in Hawaii in 1981, then committed

Rod Dixon, one of the finest distance runners ever to come out of a country known for its great runners, New Zealand, was a bronze medalist in the 1500 meters in the 1972 Olympic games. Ranked #1 in the world in the 5000 meters in 1975, he was fourth in the event at the 1976 Games. He moved on to road racing in 1980, and met with immediate success. In 1983 he ran a 2:08:59 to win the New York City Marathon, beating Great Britain's Geoff Smith in one of the most dramatic marathon finishes in the history of the sport.

Dixon was one of the first distance runners to grasp the importance of total fitness. He swims, bikes, and trains with weights regularly.

himself to training hard enough to win it the next year. He did win, becoming the only man ever to beat Dave Scott at the Ironman, and he's been winning ever since. More than that, he's one of the first guys to show the world that triathletes could race frequently—15, 20 times a year and more—and stay healthy.

There's more to it than luck. Scott Tinley's successful career is the result of a well thought out commitment that fits right into his lifestyle. The goals are set and everything is programmed in, but most important, he loves what he's doing, so that on the way to the top he's been able to accept an occasional step or two in the wrong direction and bounce back stronger than ever.

To tell you the truth, I like the guy. He's the real thing. And the message of this book is the real thing, too: nothing *has* to be done, but it *can* be done, and *will* be done if you want it to be.

Rod Dixon,
December, 1985
Los Angeles, CA

ACKNOWLEDGMENTS

Many of the quotes and excerpts that appear at the beginning of each chapter, and some of the quoted material within the book, are from articles written by Mike Plant for *Running & Triathlon News*, *Triathlon Magazine*, *Triathlete*, and *Ultrasport*.

INTRODUCTION

There aren't many triathlon experts in the world. There hasn't been time—the sport is only a few years old.

There aren't many triathlon rules, either. Who would make them, the experts?

This book does not believe in experts. *Scott Tinley's Winning Triathlon* is not likely to be referred to in years to come as "The Bible of the Sport." There aren't any commandments, there are only suggestions. You won't be told when to get up in the morning and what stretching exercises you should do on the way to the closet. What you'll read is a lot of practical information that's been gathered under fire. When John Howard tells you that "there are only two kinds of cyclists: those who have crashed and those who are going to crash," he's simply shrugging his shoulders and passing along a practical reality. An "expert" might say, "Crashing is unnecesary if you hold your hands just so on the descent and . . ."

Which is great until you crash.

If you're a seasoned triathlete, this book is probably going to remind you of a lot of things you know, but always forget to do. Or have always done, but never knew why. All of us need to constantly review the basics. One purpose of this book is to review them within the framework of one man's personal experience, so that they can be practically applied.

If you're a beginner, we hope you'll find the emphasis placed on fun and fitness in this book attractive. Not that there isn't a lot of sacrifice and hard work attached to triathlons, but why make things tougher than they have to be? A sense of humor and a healthy dose of perspective can go a long way in this sport.

Hopefully, the book will convince you to take your training one step at a time, to make the sport a part of your life rather than a disruption. And we hope, too, that you'll be encouraged every so often to pause and laugh at yourself.

By the time you finish reading the last page of the book, you should have a good working knowledge of triathlons: what they are, where they started, what the sport looks like from the inside. Whether you're serious about becoming a better triathlete, or simply *becoming* one, then you will have taken the frequent suggestions to seek supplemental information on specific topics. Most important, you will have learned to use that information wisely. If it works for you, great. If it doesn't, ignore it and move on.

There are tremendous benefits to living the triathlon lifestyle, but there are hazards, too. Zealous converts have a knack for burning themselves out or injuring themselves beyond repair. What's the use in that? Smart triathletes use their bodies well, testing them, challenging them, but with the final goal of being healthy. The "gruel-a-thon" image of the triathlon is not a popular one within the sport. If this book helps dispel that image, so much the better.

Remember that the final authority is you. We might have made this book more technical, given you more charts and graphs and performance curves, and a better definition of what a triathlete is or should be. But with the sport growing as quickly as it is, spawning technology as fast as it does, "triathlon facts" soften quickly, then collapse in a matter of months. Hopefully, much of the material you'll read on the pages that follow will be useful now and just as useful in the very unforseeable triathlon future.

Scott Tinley and Mike Plant
Encinitas, CA

SCOTT TINLEY'S WINNING TRIATHLON

"How do you feel?" a reporter asked Tom Warren toward the end of Warren's marathon at the 1979 Ironman Triathlon.

"Well," answered Warren dryly, "I don't feel like dancin'."

Julie Moss.

1
AN
UNDERGROUND
HISTORY

In the minds of most of the world, the sport of triathlon was born on February 22, 1982, on the Big Island of Hawaii. That was the year I won the race, and I wish I could say that Scott Tinley was what all the excitement was about. He wasn't. What everyone will remember in years to come is the dramatic finish of the women's event, with Julie Moss collapsing yards from the finish line and Kathleen McCartney running by her to take first place. ABC television cameras were right on top of it, and when the scene was aired on "Wide World of Sports," with the haunting sounds of Tim Weisberg's flute in the background, tears rolled down the cheeks of Americans everywhere. Julie, red hair, freckles, and all, was an unlikely heroine, but her performance touched all the right buttons for that very reason. She was the girl next door who had taken and just barely passed the most grueling test of all. If she could do it, so could anyone else. Even if you thought the whole idea of the Ironman was crazy, you weren't likely to forget the word *triathlon* very soon.

Kathleen McCartney recalled her own feelings being affected by Julie's effort: ". . . it wasn't until I got to the last half-mile that the crowd wasn't cheering. They'd just gone through something very emotional with Julie. They'd seen a girl totally fall apart. She'd stolen their hearts. I remember feeling almost a bewilderment. I was just running, not thinking of anything in particular except trying to get to the finish line as fast as I could. I didn't interact with the crowd at that point. It was dark, and there were these really bright lights at the finish. I remember seeing shadows and heads and faces and hearing sounds. I sensed a different feeling in the crowd than I'd felt in crowds before. I didn't know what was going on at the time, but now, in retrospect, I can feel how the crowd's mood must have been affected. . . .

"It was a bittersweet victory. Hearts were torn. . . ."

It's understandable, then, why many people, even many within the sport of triathlon, automatically associate the Ironman with the first days of the sport. Actually, though, triathlons are rooted in southern California—in San Diego, to be exact—where running, cycling, and swimming all on the same day was never a cruel test of the human will to endure; it's always been a way of life.

The early triathletes in San Diego were runners looking for an alternative to the weekend 10K. After a hard run, the best way to cool off was a dip in the ocean or Mission Bay; it was inevitable that someone would put the two sports together.

David Pain, a San Diego lawyer who had earlier been instrumental in founding the Masters running movement, was certainly one of the first to do so, at least officially. In 1972, he threw a party in his own honor and called it the David Pain Birthday Biathlon. The race consisted of a 6.2-mile run and a half-mile swim. Two years later, a couple of friends of his, two fellow members of the San Diego Track Club, Don Shannahan and Jack Johnstone, added a bike ride to Pain's combination, and the sport was born. While it is probably true that a bike ride of more than 20 miles or a swim longer than a mile would have scared most of the early guys to death, at least the ball was rolling.

Shannahan's and Johnstone's Mission Bay Triathlon, centered around Fiesta Island in San Diego, was probably the first organized run/bike/swim triathlon in the world, although the term *organized* should be interpreted loosely. There were no bike racks, numbers, tri-suits, or mile markers. The very essence of the event was informality.

The winner of that first event, for the record, was a 46-year-old exercise physiologist at San Diego State University named Bill Phillips. The distances: a 2.8-mile run, a 5-mile bike ride, a quarter-mile swim, a 2-mile run, and a quarter-mile swim. The first Ironman was four years away, rumblings of the sport's mass popularity six years down the road. Becoming a "triathlete" was the furthest thing from anyone's mind.

"No one ever trained for those things," remembers Phillips. "They were a change of pace. I was running well at the time, and I'd been a swimmer in college, so I had an advantage. All I had to do was stay close on the run. You couldn't lose much ground on a five-mile bike, and no one else could swim."

Phillips just laughs when I remind him that he is a historical figure—the winner of the first triathlon. "Yeah, that'll get me a cup of coffee one day."

The first triathlon I ever saw was one of Shannahan's and Johnstone's masterpieces on Fiesta Island in July 1976. I wasn't sure exactly what was going on—I'd never even *heard* of a triathlon—but I thought it looked like fun, so I asked when the next race was going to be held. Sometime in August, I was told, so I kept my eyes on the race schedule in the *San Diego Track Club Newsletter* and showed up a month later on a Wednesday night at 5:00 P.M. ready to go.

I didn't have any idea of what to expect. I probably wouldn't today, either, because the course still consisted pretty much of the same distances they'd begun with. It was more of an obstacle course than a triathlon.

Having plenty of running experience, I went off with the leaders. Tom Warren, who would go on to win the 1979 Ironman in Hawaii, was there, and so were the Buckingham brothers, Wally and Wayne.

Wally (front) and Wayne
Buckingham of San
Diego wear the original
Tri-Suit: swim trunks
and goggles.

The Buckinghams were identical twins who ran for a hot local running club called the Jamul Toads. The "Toads," as they were locally referred to, once were winners of the National AAU Cross Country Championship, and although neither brother ran as part of that championship team, they were still fast. The Buckinghams ran 10Ks consistently under 30 minutes, and since they were both San Diego city lifeguards, they could swim, too. That August afternoon, they led the field going into the bike ride.

I was in third or fourth behind them, and I'll never forget my very first transition. I got on the bike, which was a huge, 25-inch SR Gran Course. It weighed a good 30 pounds, with thick, clincher tires, saddlebags, and those cruiser brakes with the double levers so you can ride sitting up. I was riding in tennis shorts, of course, and running shoes, but as bad as I was, the Buckingham brothers were even worse.

I caught them on the second loop around Fiesta Island and came off the bike maybe 30 seconds ahead. My swimming was pretty poor then, and as soon as I went into the water I cramped up. The Buckinghams passed me, but I made it out of the water and decided to follow them. I had no idea of what the exact course was. They ran along the shore, then went back into the water, and I followed right along. Then we came out and ran some more, then *swam* some more. On

Chuck's Triathlon was a late version of the early Fiesta Island triathlon first put on in the early '70s by the San Diego Track Club. The emphasis, at first, was on team competition and the atmosphere was very, very informal.

the last swim I went into the water right behind Wally, only to be passed by Warren, who came by me about three-quarters of the way across. Only he didn't just go by me. He stopped, gave me a toothy, I-told-you-so grin, then swam on. I'd never met the guy before, but I never forgot him after that race—more than three years before his win in Hawaii and the Ironman article by Barry McDermott in *Sports Illustrated* that turned so many people on to this sport.

I was third in that first race, which was not a bad way to start my triathlon career, but what I remember most was the spontaneity of the event, the camaraderie of the people, the craziness. No one then was under the impression that we were onto anything more than a great way to have fun. We worked hard—everyone out there was by nature extremely competitive—but it was all very basic. You showed up on Wednesday night, paid your buck, and then wobbled through the course as well as you could. Your bike was the same machine you used to run down to the store or cruise the beach on Sunday afternoon after your long run in the morning.

By August 1976, several triathlon or triathlonlike events were being held in the San Diego area. The San Diego Track Club had added a team triathlon to the Fiesta Island schedule, and Coronado Island, home of a big naval base and the famous Del Coronado Hotel, was hosting its third annual Coronado Optimist Triathlon.

One of the first competitors in the Coronado race was Chief Warrant Officer Moki Martin, a pioneer in San Diego triathlons and the originator of one of the first half-Ironman-distance events ever held: the Super Frog Triathlon, which is still held today, although it is largely restricted to military personnel. A fine triathlete in the mid- and late-'70s, Martin is no longer able to compete; he was partially paralyzed in a freak head-on bicycle collision in 1982. He is, however, able to swim three times a week, and he still puts in some time on a stationary bicycle.

In 1974, Martin was a member of the elite naval combat group, the SEALs, and he was fascinated by multisport events. (SEAL is an acronym for Sea, Air, and Land, denoting the group's combat versatility.) He felt that the triathlon format—especially the swim-run combination—was particularly applicable to SEAL training.

"It was what we were doing, anyway," Martin remembers. "All of our training was like that, although I felt that the way we were approaching it was not the best way. Our routine was a lot of calisthenics followed by long beach runs on the sand with boondockers [combat boots] and combat gear. There were a lot of injuries: knee problems, shin problems."

By 1976, Martin was a lieutenant junior grade and a SEAL training officer. He put triathlon principles to work on his men, combining swimming and running over shorter distances in rapid succession to build stamina and reduce injuries. At the same time, he quietly began to encourage some of his SEALs to enter local triathlons.

"Our guys thought they were tough," says Martin, "but competing in the other events showed them that there was a whole other world out there that was a lot tougher in mind and body than they were. One event that was always a good one to go to was Tom Warren's Swim/Run/Swim. The SEALs were taught to swim 'no-splash' strokes, like sidestroke, for combat. They got halfway around the pier in Tom's race, and they just about died! They weren't in shape to swim that far using the crawl."

The race Martin was referring to was one of the most organized of the early San Diego events. It wasn't a triathlon, but it set the stage for a lot that was going to come later. Tug's Tavern Run/Swim/Run was the brainchild of Tom Warren, who owned Tug's, a San Diego beach area bar where you could eat cheap Mexican breakfasts in the morning and drink whatever kind of beer you like all day. (Tug's closed with great fanfare in November, 1985.)

Tom was one of the world's first triathletes without even knowing it. He was a competitive swimmer in college, and as a kid in San Diego he'd learned to use his bike for just about everything, from delivering papers to transporting his surfboard. There's nothing special about either one of those things, except that as Tom grew up, he was constantly on the edge of doing something crazy that involved one of the two sports, with running thrown in for good measure. He'd bike to Mexico to have a drink at a certain bar, or he'd bet some guy that he could swim from here to there despite the fact that it had never been done. Along the way, he picked up a lot of endurance and a lot of knowledge about his own personal limits.

"When I was a newspaper boy," Tom says, "I rode a bike one hour a morning, 365 days a year for seven years, so I should have picked up *something*. I used to

Tug's Tavern Swim/Run/Swim, put on by Tom Warren, took place in San Diego's Pacific Beach. First held in 1975, it was one of the early multisport events and typified the southern California lifestyle.

be able to carry my whole Sunday load all at once—a hundred pounds. Every once in a while it was too heavy, and I'd go around in circles. I could never straighten the bike up. I'd have to get off and pull the front end around."

A big thing with Tom was having his friends get involved in his workouts, and that was pretty much the way the Tug's race began in 1976. Although the course varied a little each year, it was generally a short run followed by a half-mile swim around Crystal Pier (at the base of Garnet Avenue in Pacific Beach), a five-mile run down to the Mission Beach jetty and back, a return swim around the pier,

TOM WARREN—A TRIATHLON ORIGINAL

In 30 years or so, when triathlon has grown up and settled into its rightful place in the world of international sport, a group of important-looking middle-aged men and women in dark suits—policy makers in big-time triathlon—will sit in a hotel bar in some exotic European city after a marathon session of negotiations and laugh about the humble beginnings of the sport. They'll talk about the early races and the early crazies who populated them. Without a doubt, one of the people they'll talk about will be the biggest crazy of all, Tom Warren.

Warren is the Ty Cobb, the Walter Johnson, the Dizzy Dean of triathlons. He is a character of legendary proportions, not really because of what he did, but because of the way he did it. He is a Grand Philosopher whose podium is as likely to be a bar stool as a bicycle seat.

Physically, Warren is an odd assortment of spare parts. His arms and legs are knobby and gnarled, and his chin, highlighted by a walrus moustache, is constantly competing with his barrel chest for top billing at the front. It's been said he runs like a duck, but that's too simple. Running along the water's edge in Pacific Beach, Warren resembles nothing so much as a tough, weathered old shore bird, crumpled years ago by a big wave he didn't see.

A former competitive swimmer and water polo player at the University of Southern California, Warren won the second ever Ironman Triathlon in 1979, competing against 14 others in weather awful enough to close down half of the island of Oahu. Since then, he's stayed close to the event, grumbling about its growing commercialism and fading sense of competitive

Tom Warren.

fairness and camaraderie, but competing nonetheless. His best finishes were a second place in 1980, third in '81, then a 10th place in February 1982.

Warren is at his best when he is talking about his early days in San Diego as an endurance athlete—a passion he would have pursued whether Ironman or triathlons had come along or not. He sets his goals in big clumps, then goes about achieving them methodically, with an eye always open for a side issue here or there that might add to the experience.

That's kind of the way Warren talks, too—plenty of side issues along the way toward the ultimate goal. He's fascinating, frenetic, and philosophical, but never boring; he's almost Casey Stengel-ish in his delivery. You nod your head like crazy while he's talking, because everything makes perfect sense—until you realize you're not sure exactly what it was you heard. Warren is a piece of triathlon history far removed from your new pink $2,000 bike and your high-tech computer shoes. I can't vouch for the 100 percent accuracy of what follows, but the look at triathlon history through the eyes of one of the sport's real characters is irresistible:

ST: Tell me about the early, early triathlons. Where did the whole thing begin?

Warren: A lot of it was the San Diego Track Club. What happened is a lot of track club members would start riding the bike as an experiment to recover from injuries. Some of them did some swimming, too, and then they decided to have a little race, a team race. I remember Bill Gookin [a past president of the San Diego Track Club and the inventor of ERG, an early electrolyte replacement drink] was in it because he almost drowned, literally drowned. I mean they had to pluck him out of the water. When I finally entered one, they'd had a couple of races already, although I was gonna do the first one.

ST: This was what, mid '70s?

Warren: Well, I think it was '72. The only reason I think that is because I was gonna do a 15-mile ocean swim or do the triathlon. This girlfriend of mine, Jeanie, had heard about the triathlon in one of her classes at San Diego State, and she said, "Hey, you gotta do this; they're gonna have this triathlon—it's a natural for you." See, I was doing a lot of ocean swims—I'd do the La Jolla Rough Water Swim, then I'd run afterward, and I'd already ridden the bike to Cabo San Lucas and stuff, so I *had* the background. But see, it was on the same day as this 15-mile ocean swim, and my goal was to swim the Catalina Channel. So I went ahead and did the ocean race instead, so I know they must have had a triathlon in 1972.

ST: So you did the race the next year?

Warren: It was maybe the second time they'd done it, and they had publicized it as a straight one-mile swim, so me and my friend Mike O'Conner, a bartender at the Brigantine, entered. Well, he's a seven-and-a-half-minute miler at best, maybe eight-minute, but I had never gotten worse than third in any rough water swim up and down the coast, and I didn't know anyone in San Diego who could beat me, so I was stoked. I figured we could win the race even with him running.

ST: So, did you win?

Warren: Well, see, we get there, and they had made it six short swims instead of a one-mile swim. We got 13th, and I got it in my head that those people had changed the race to accommodate themselves, so I was pissed and started training for triathlons.

ST: What was the format of the race then?

Warren: We'd run from the entrance of Fiesta Island down to Sea World and back, then the next guy would bike two short loops around Fiesta Island. Then the first guy would do a swim/run/swim where he'd swim out across the cove to that little island, run 20 feet, swim again, then run down the beach 100 yards and come across. . . . See, so you did all these little broken up swims, and that's when I thought that, if they'd let me swim a straight mile, I would have *killed* those guys, see? And then the last guy ran the big loop around the island—4.2 miles—and that was the end of the race. The second year I did it with Bill Phillips, and we ended up winning. Then I think we won it the next year. . . .

ST: How did you meet up with Phillips?

Warren: Well, what I did is win this race called the Clear Lake Marathon, up near Sacramento in California. You'd run seven miles, then you swam three miles in the lake, then you ran through a parking lot and everything, then you got into these pear orchards where there were no trails, and you followed these markers. You ran up to the top of this mountain, and at that point they had a little check station with these little old people with a cup of coffee and a walkie-talkie. You told them your number, and there was a trophy for whoever got there first. Then you'd run down the mountain and swim another three miles. That was in '74, maybe '73—I have the trophies at home, so I can tell ya.

Well, Phillips read that in *Sports Illustrated*, and he called me up and asked if he could come down and train with me. He was a physiologist up at San Diego State, but I didn't know that, so I taught him physiology for about a year and a half, not knowing. We'd do these swim/runs all over Mission Bay in San Diego. He was a better runner than me but I could *always* run much better than him out of the water, so I'd tell him: "The reason is your blood flow is . . . and you don't know how to move your arms. . . ." And all the time he's a coach and a physiologist, but I never bothered to ask him, you know?

The way I finally found out after about a year and a half was I was telling him how this Indian tribe—the Tamara-mara or whatever they are—would kick this ball, and I told him the whole story, see? And he kept saying, "Yeah, we . . . yeah, we . . . ," and finally when he said "we" I said, "Whattaya mean, 'we'?" and it turns out he was one of the guys who did the film that I watched!

So that's how I met him. I used to take him around Mission Bay and get him lost. He'd just follow me all over, and we'd do that twice a week. And I'd get him to bodysurf with me and stuff.

ST: When did you start incorporating biking into your training—or *whatever* you were doing?

Warren: I did biking before that . . . like when I was 20 years old I rode to Tijuana on my bike a *lot*. I remember riding at midnight once, getting there at three in the morning or something—on a three-speed with a six-pack of beer on my handlebars—and dancin' at the Aloha Club and getting a ride home at 6:30 in the morning. And then going for a swim.

My longest ride was with David Manwaring and those guys. [Manwaring, from San Diego, founded in the early '70s a mass bike ride that went from Tecate, Mexico, to Ensenada, Mexico, a distance of approximately 75 miles. Thousands now participate each year.] What they were doing was prepping for the long ride. Every week they'd do longer and longer rides, and I was telling them that I could do the ride without all the training. Their big ride was to Ramona—50 miles was what they said. So I said to this bar manager of mine, "Hey, we'll leave before them and get there and just wait for them." He said, "Fine," and we were all set.

I had a 21-inch Raleigh with the handlebars turned up and I went down to the bar and set everything up for the day, and then we headed out about 9:00. Those other guys were leaving at 10:30 or something. I didn't have toe clips or anything, so what I did was I made 'em out of baling wire. It was perfect for a tennis shoe, you know? Then I covered the seat with bar rags with rubber bands on 'em for my butt and we took off.

It really wasn't hard for me at all—it was like I'd always done it, but my friend got some bad cramps going up the big hills. Finally, we got to this roadside bar just outside of Ramona where I knew Manwaring's group always stopped. We went in there and quick ordered a drink, see, because we wanted to be drinking when they showed up. Then we had three or four, and suddenly our money was gone. Luckily, the bartender knew them, and he said "Look, I'll give you credit." So we started shooting pool, and pretty soon it was about three o'clock, and we don't know what to do—we don't know how to get home. Finally, they walk in. What had happened was they had scheduled a picnic in Ramona with girls and everything. . . . And then the guy in the bar said, "Let's make this good," meaning our bar bill, and he points to the bar. We were the only ones there the whole day, and the entire bar was covered with empty beer bottles—like eight cases of beer! We owed about twenty bucks each.

ST: You had a reputation then for working out in the sauna or something, didn't you?

Warren: I used to do that, yeah. I met this guy once at Mulvaney's [a beach-area restaurant and bar in San Diego] after that ride to Ramona with Manwaring, named Embry or something. He'd been on the ride, and we got to talking, so I told him I did this maintenance program—this was *way* before the triathlons. I'd go down to Mission Bay and swim a mile, sit in the Jacuzzi, then I'd go out and run around the Mission Bay track, then I'd go over and do a run/swim/run back in the bay. Then I'd do my sit-ups in the sauna. See, sitting in there, trying to lose weight, I'd get real bored, so I'd start doing sit-ups. After a while I could do 400. I'd win beers all the time on bets. My butt had a big callus on it from doing them. So this guy Embry I was talking to says, "Hey, I'll do that with ya," but I hadn't told him about the sauna.

So this guy Embry takes a look after we'd done all that other stuff, and he says, "A deal's a deal," so he's in there doing 'em with me. This is like 8:30, 9:00 at night. Finally he runs out, and I can hear him throwin' up behind the sauna. Later on he's giving me this crap about doing my workout, and I go, "Yup, gaggghgh, gaggghgh. . . ." He said, "Gee, I didn't know you *heard* that!" He ended up making national cycling teams and traveling all over the world.

ST: You used to have a lot of fun on those Tecate-Ensenada rides, didn't you?

Warren: Oh, I remember this one time—'70, '71 I think—it was the hottest day on record in August in San Diego County, and I was worried about getting sunburned. You didn't really worry about as many things then as you do now, but I didn't want to get sunburned, so we bought these cowboy hats, and the wind was blowin' so you couldn't keep the hat on while you were riding, so I took a bunji cord and hooked it under my chin, so then you couldn't *talk*, see? I remember the thing flippin' off and shootin' 20 feet in the air one time.

ST: What was the first individual triathlon you remember? Those early ones were for teams.

Warren: That was down at Fiesta Island, too. I think I got second. I know I didn't win it. I do remember being totally confused and not knowing where we were going.

ST: What about the Navy SEALs? Didn't they get involved pretty early?

Warren: No, later. There were a couple of races in Coronado. They had one where they had the Coronado Half Marathon and then an ocean swim that afternoon, and they added the two together. That's when I met [John] Dunbar—in '78—and he said, "You gotta do the Ironman!" That's when I first decided to go to Hawaii.

Then there was the Hard Rock Triathlon.

ST: I won that once.

Warren: Must have been after me.

ST: It was. They had the Coronado 10K as the first event, right? And then on the following day . . .

Warren: No, that afternoon you had to swim a half-mile, and then the following day they had a little triathlon that started on the bike. You were seeded according to how fast you got your entry in. I always got seeded number one. I won it five years in a row. The Optimists Club put it on and those guys would personally deliver my entry 'cause what they wanted to do was come up and drink beer at Tug's. They liked me 'cause I was old—I'll betcha I was just 30, 32 . . .

ST: Now that's an old race.

Warren: Oh, real old.

ST: Four-mile bike, quarter-mile swim . . .

Warren: And you could draft.

ST: And a one-mile run.

Warren: And you could draft. I'm sure I've still got the record, 'cause I did the whole race in 22 minutes once—the swim was only 150 yards. My philosophy was . . . see, I knew all those guys could outrun me, so what I had to do was get them real tired in the first 200 yards, so in my training every day I'd do 10 repeats of this big hill next to my house and 10 repeats across De Anza Cove swimming. Then I think I rode up and down the boardwalk some, and then I'd run up my stairs with ankle weights 20 times. When I got to the top on the last one, I would run as fast as I could down that little hallway in my house. I did that every day.

ST: There aren't too many races like that any more. The sport is sophisticated now. Do you miss the old days?

Warren: Well, there's two people in me. In a way, some of it's ruined. But it's great, because the way it is now is the only way a lot of people can get involved. It's kind of selfish to think that I'm the only one who is supposed to enjoy this thing.

But I always got a sense of accomplishment by doing something out of the norm, see? If I took Scott Tinley's training and did *that*, then I wouldn't be doing anything out of the norm.

People *approach* it wrong. I don't think they get as much out of it. They should have more fun, be more adventuresome. They train by the book, whatever they think the book is. But there stilll *isn't* a book—might never be.

They get so *addicted*. If you don't ride, run, and swim every day, you're in trouble. I don't think that's good.

and a run up the beach to the finish line. In the tradition of the race—and of the early San Diego triathlon scene in general—the best part of the morning for a lot of the competitors was the tortilla-and-bean breakfast served up after all the excitement. I've been competing in the Tug's event for years, but only in 1985 did I finally win it. The victory will sit very close to my heart for a long time—because of the history of the race, because of its local flavor, and because of Tom.

How far the sport of triathlon would have gone had it stayed within the laid-back San Diego format is impossible to guess. Perhaps the expansion was inevitable, considering the kind of people who were involved. In any case, a lot of the impetus for creating an event far beyond the scope of the first, tiny Mission Bay Triathlons certainly came from San Diego; in particular, the damned-if-I-can't-do-it San Diego SEAL team connection.

The Ironman in Hawaii was the key that opened the triathlon door. Navy lieutenant John Collins and John Dunbar (who as a SEAL had competed in multisport events in San Diego along with Moki Martin) began talking about putting together the triathlon of triathlons on the island of Oahu in 1977. The next year it happened, with Dunbar placing second and word of the event finding its way back to San Diego. Tom Warren, for one, couldn't resist. He flew to Hawaii the following February and became the Ironman, finishing ahead of 11 others. Fifteen had started. Dunbar again was second. The difference this time, though, was the presence of a *Sports Illustrated* writer who went home and told the world about an event that no one in his right mind would ever want to do. No one that is, except. . . .

All across the country, triathletes-to-be read McDermott's description of Warren's survival, of Dunbar bouncing off parked cars in fatigue, and vowed to do the race. In 1980 more than 100 did. Then, in '81, there were more than 300 finishers in Hawaii, and smaller races utilizing the same swim/bike/run format cropped up in dozens of cities back on the mainland. The sport was on its way.

". . . [Mark] Allen, in his orange and black Team J David skinsuit, was first out of the bike lot. [Scott] Molina had beaten him out of the water by almost ten seconds, but Allen's teammate took an almost casual change. Sitting on the ground calmly tying his shoes, Molina was an island of composure in a scene rapidly filling with the controlled chaos of a triathlon transition area. Dave Scott struggled into his clothes and flew off in pursuit, then Dean Harper did the same. Announcements came in rapid French over the public address system, adding to the intensity of the moment. Jann Girard came out of the water fifth overall, but Linda Buchanan was only 45 seconds behind and Jenny Lamott was literally at Buchanan's heels. Suddenly, the elegance and culture of the Mediterranean setting was gone, forgotten. The athletes headed west frantically along the Promenade des Anglais, but it might have been Main St., USA. Quickly, quickly, tie the shoes, grab a drink and go. Up ahead were 75 miles of hard riding. Up ahead was a shot at ten thousand green American dollars."—The 1983 Nice, France, Triathlon

2
LIFE IN THE PITS

What makes the triathlon different from other sports? The unique physical challenge is a factor, but there are triathlons of many distances today, some more intimidating than others. An event that takes less than two hours for a triathlete to complete is a very different race from the awesome, full-day survival ritual of the Ironman.

Both races, however, have the complex technical considerations of the triathlon in common. Perhaps that's one reason why the sport has become so popular in the technologically conscious '80s. Instead of merely man against the elements, it's man and equipment—goggles and wet suits, wheels and gears and spokes—against the course, the other triathletes, whatever the race throws at them. And where it all comes together—where the men and women and machinery meet and shift and intermingle—is the transition area, that unique element of the triathlon that makes the sport a creature unto itself.

The situation is obvious and unavoidable—every competitor in a triathlon is competing in three sports, and he or she must move from one to another with a minimal period of adjustment. There isn't a whole lot of time to think—you just act. The rapid-fire "life in the pits" is what makes the triathlon different. The transition area, where swimmers become cyclists and cyclists become runners, where photographers shoot their best pictures and friends and families get to glimpse close up the frenzy of competition, is the heart and soul of the sport.

The history of triathlons is reflected very clearly in the athletes' changing attitudes toward transitions. In the old days, moving from one sport to another just for fun on a clear, sunny day in San Diego was, by definition, leisurely. Then running, biking, and swimming, one right after another, became an organized

Man and machinery meet in the triathlon transition area.

Transition areas in the early races were wherever your assistant was standing. It was exciting, confusing, and, as the fields grew larger, dangerous.

sport, and the procedure became more defined. Certain athletes developed techniques that other athletes copied, but no routine remained standard for very long.

Back when the sport was just getting off the ground—in the mid-'70s— transitions were quick, mostly due to the fact that the races were short. We did everything in our swimsuits, cycled in our running shoes, and wore our goggles around our necks or on our heads so that they'd be ready for the final swim leg. Bike racks were nonexistent, of course, but handlers were allowed to hold our bikes and help us change.

When longer races started being held a couple of years later, the goggles on the heads disappeared. Cycling shorts on the bike replaced swimsuits. There was more equipment involved, but we were still in the dark ages. Transitions took forever. Everyone was still thinking "endurance" instead of "speed." Warren, for instance, was known for his precise and methodical preparation. At the Horny Toad Triathlon in 1980, he came out of the water, rinsed off, then sat down on a curb with his cycling gear laid out in front of him like an elaborate picnic spread. There were even spare socks and extra shoelaces. He took five minutes at least to change, talking with his support crew about strategy all the while. That kind of methodical preparation today would cost Warren five or six places in the final standings.

THE HISTORY OF TRANSITIONS

Here's a brief historical transition chronology. Having been a part of the evolution, I find the changes in attitude and the changes in equipment fascinating:

1978

This was the year in which runners realized that they could go faster on a bike if they wore cleated cycling shoes. A new dimension was added to the sport—if you couldn't deal with more than one pair of shoelaces in a single day, you were in big trouble.

1979

Comfort became a factor. Cycling shorts appeared, replacing Speedos in the shorter races and cutoffs in the longer ones. That necessitated a third change, from cycling shorts and shoes to running gear, and a corresponding shift in acceptable competitive modesty went along with the new arrangement. Exposure of bare bottoms (to the delight of eager newspaper photographers) predated the introduction of changing tents by several months. Coverage by the major networks (or fear of uncoverage, to be more exact) prompted race directors to supply competitors with private areas in which to switch clothing.

1980

Organization—Tom Warren style—was the rage. Planning and preparation were recognized as prerequisites to speed, and cute little innovations like foot baths to rinse salt water and sand off the triathletes' feet began to appear.

1981

As interest in the sport grew and fields became larger and larger, race directors were forced to keep individual support crews off the roads. No longer was it possible to have assistants hand triathletes their bikes after the swim, although many race directors learned this the hard way. One of the holdouts was the Rusty Pelican Triathlon in Newport Beach, where the bike-to-run transition area (the swim was last) was little more than a narrow aisle of hundreds of screaming bike handlers through which triathletes had to fight. The necessity paved the way for the invention: bike racks made their appearance.

Race directors were forced to limit the press's access to courses, too, but most photographers had by this time come to realize that being in a transition area was much more exciting than being out on the course, anyway.

The good viewing also attracted family and friends. With that in mind, the Bud Light Ironman Triathlon in Hawaii erected grandstands in the transition areas. Spectators didn't have to pay for the seats, but it would have been standing room only even if they had.

The swimmers swim while the bikes wait in the transition area of the Chicago Bud Light USTS Triathlon.
COURTESY BUD LIGHT USTS

Nineteen eighty-one also saw the introduction of the tri-suit, an innovation that was viewed with much skepticism at first. Could you swim in the things? In fact, you could, and they offered plenty of available space for sponsor logos, too, a feature that Dave Horning, an early winner of the Escape from Alcatraz Triathlon and a notorious self-promoter, noticed before anyone else. A lot of people followed Horning's lead as more and more triathletes sought financial assistance to subsidize their training.

1982

Prize money was offered for the first time in 1982, and slow transitions became more than a matter of injured pride—they cost you money. In many instances, triathletes won races or lost places (and dollars) by seconds lost or gained in changing areas.

Athletes began to train with transitions in mind, practicing their transition routines step by step, trying to shave what had become precious seconds off their total time.

1983

Triathlon race direction became a complex science, with some directors failing miserably, others shining. The toughest part of all was setting up a workable transition area for hundreds of triathletes. The large fields forced race directors to think about flow patterns, portable bike racks, unique shower systems, and aid stations that could service traffic moving in three directions at once.

On the competitive side, triathletes were being forced to make strategic decisions that would have seemed ridiculous less than two years before. Shower or not? Change clothes or wear a tri-suit? Drink on the way out or drink on the run? The sport was heating up, and the flurry of activity in the transition area was the flash point.

How important had fast transitions become by 1983? Well, Dave Scott won the Bud Light Ironman Triathlon in October. He set a course record by finishing in 9 hours, 5 minutes, and 57 seconds, winning the race for the third time and cementing his place in triathlon history. I placed second, all of 33 seconds behind him. It would be silly to say that I would have won the race had I been a little quicker coming out of the swim or slightly faster going from the bike to the run, but it sure gives you something to think about, doesn't it?

Julie Moss struggles with a bike shoe and keeps her eye on the competition at the same time.

1984

Fast transitions became almost an art form, as short races, like those of the Bud Light US Triathlon Series, became more sophisticated, more competitive, and more profitable. Clothing and equipment manufacturers tried to keep up. Tri-suits were used widely, one shoe company introduced the first high-tech running shoes with a Velcro closing system instead of lacing (they were too heavy to become widely popular), and another outfitted a women's team with a prototype, legless racing suit for short-distance events. Neither idea caught on, but it was the thought that counted. Triathletes, born in the image of the rugged individualist with nothing between himself or herself and the impossible but a strong mind and a hard body, were suddenly, as one writer put it, "the high-tech super-jocks of the '80s."

1985, '86, and beyond

Mass participation in the sport of triathlon will continue to increase and fuel the shorter-distance races. Transitions will become more important in the future, and the technology of the sport will reflect that. Just as tri-suits have made the act of changing clothes a thing of the past, so will shoes with removable, interchangeable soles conquer the problem of moving from the bike to the run. Even tri-suits will undergo further evolution, perhaps adopting peel-away arms and legs for racing when the mornings are cold and the afternoons hot.

Spectator interest will grow, too, along with the popularity of the short-distance events. The key? Transition areas, of course. To accommodate spectators, race directors will loop competitors several times past the central staging area. Big races, where top pros compete and big money is on the line, might even charge for tickets for seats close to the transition areas and all the action. If spectator interest goes even further, we may see triathlons staged in outdoor arenas, with a velodrome and a running track and 50,000 screaming triathlon fans rooting for the hometown favorite.

It might sound farfetched now, but the idea of 1,000 people doing the Bud Light Ironman—and 6,000 more trying to get in—was equally improbable just a few short years ago.

TRANSITION TIPS

Training

It's important to simulate race conditions occasionally. If you're not racing frequently, come back from a bike ride and go out immediately and run. I wouldn't recommend it more than several times a month, however, because the constant abuse of back-to-back training puts a tremendous strain on your system. Better to relax for an hour or so after your ride, rehydrate and stretch before running, or vice versa. You may find, like many triathletes have, myself included, that cycling after running will cut down on the injuries.

No time to waste!

Stretching is important. A good stretching program is the best way to improve your ability to go smoothly and efficiently from one sport to another. It's understood that there are only so many hours in the day for training, and if anything is easy to leave out, it's stretching. But the 15 minutes or so a day a simple routine takes may save the precious hours you've put in on the roads from being wasted due to injury.

Competition

Toward the end of the swim—the last 20 yards or so—switch from the freestyle to the breaststroke. Not only will this allow you to get your bearings on exactly where the swim ends; it will also loosen up your legs and knees and allow the blood to flow into those extremities.

Toward the end of the bike:

Do the little things *before* **the race.**

- Shift to an easier gear and spin your pedals for 30 seconds to a minute, two to three times, to loosen up your calves and thighs.
- Stand up on your pedals to get blood moving into your feet. Stretch at this point, too. Three good end-of-ride stretches:
  1. Press your heels down and straighten your legs alternately to stretch out your calves.
  2. Put both pedals parallel to the ground and press your hips forward to loosen up your lower back.
  3. With the pedals still parallel to the ground, rock forward and stretch your gluteals.

Tricks of the Trade

- Use a water bucket to rinse sand off your feet after the swim. This will prevent blisters and sore feet from chafing.
- Set your bike in an easy gear before the swim so you don't have to grunt and groan getting it out of the transition area.
- Have all your gear laid out neatly, within easy reach, but don't spread it out so other competitors will kick it around.

Organization is the key. Of course, you can go too far. Experience will tell you where you can cut corners in the transition area and still get by.

Lace locks cut shoe-tying time to a minimum.

- The fewer clothes, the better.
- Use lace-locks or Velcro closures for your cycling and running shoes. Shoelaces take too long to tie.
- Put your feet in the toe clips after you are underway—don't wobble around in the transition area trying to get them in.

Tri-Suits or Not?

I personally don't use them. In a short race, I ride in my running shorts or just my swimsuit. Keep a little gob of petroleum jelly beneath your seat and apply it while you're riding—that should solve the chafing problem.

In longer races, the comfort of dry, padded bike shorts and the convenience of being able to carry food in the back pockets outweigh the time savings possible with tri-suits.

If you do wear a tri-suit, get a good one that fits. A loose fit or poor-quality tri-suit will create drag in the water.

Save time where you can— change on the run where possible, because time is a lot easier to gain (and lose) in the transition area than on the road.

The Importance of Time

There are no time standards for transitions, because each race has its own way of timing them. Some start the watch when you enter from one end and stop it when you leave your position at the bike rack; others start the watch when you come in, then don't stop it until you leave the entire area. Some don't time transitions at all. And different races require different things of the competitors, like long runs from the water to the bike. Generally, though, anything under two minutes is good for either the swim-to-bike change or the bike-to-run. The best triathletes are much faster than that—for good reason.

Consider: 2 minutes in the transition area can go by very quickly. But over the course of a 10K running race, 2 minutes translate into a difference of 20 seconds per mile—the difference between a 6-minute mile and a 5:40!

Give me a choice, and I'll try to make up those two minutes in the transition area any day!

Things Not to Do

Watch where you're going in the transition area. There's a lot going on. Keep your eyes open and your head up. Don't take chances. You're liable to put yourself and a competitor out of the race.

Be fair. Many triathletes, even ones who have been around long enough to know better, throw their bikes around where they will be in the way of other competitors, or they scatter the equipment of the athletes on either side of them trying to get to their own stuff.

Lastly, try to keep your mind working—at least a little. I lost a lot of time in a race in Los Angeles in 1985 by rushing into the transition area after the bike ride, racking my bike, and then spending *at least* 20 seconds looking for my shoes. I finally found them—underneath the rear wheel of my bike. I lost the race by—you guessed it—20 seconds.

"Triathlon transition areas are normally places of frantic, uncontrolled activity and excitement, where athletes dive in and out of equipment with panicked urgency. Not so with the Malibu Triathlon.

"The cold waters off Zuma Beach took a terrible toll. Out of a select field of 75 top triathletes, 19 had to be pulled from the water by lifeguards. Twelve more had to be helped to hot showers and were disqualified for receiving aid. The survivors hobbled to their bicycles and in awful silence tried to make the change. Their routines, practiced many times in triathlon after triathlon, would have normally taken a minute or two. This time, they struggled for five or ten, while boyfriends and girlfriends, wives and husbands, like managers of prize fighters taking savage beatings, were constantly on the verge of throwing in the towel and taking their athlete home in one piece, at least. 'Stay down!' their concerned faces seemed to be saying. 'Stay down!'

"But after a mile and a half swim in 57-degree water, few of the triathletes who had made it to their bikes were willing to quit. *Ready* to quit, yes, but not willing. After all, they were the lucky ones. Some of the best people in the sport hadn't even made it that far."—The 1982 Malibu Triathlon

3
THE SWIM

Whenever I think about the 1982 Malibu Triathlon, I think of swimming. They aren't pleasant memories. I don't think that anyone who competed in that race has good thoughts about any part of it, but the swim was the worst—a long mile and a half in sub-60-degree water.

Malibu was the first professional triathlon—the first race to offer prize money in substantial amounts. I can still feel the chill, standing on the beach with a field of other top triathletes just three weeks after Ironman in the fog and the drizzle, listening to race director Hans Albrecht tell us that the water had been "hovering around 65 degrees all week." That might have been true, but it had stopped hovering the night before the race and started nose-diving toward 57. None of us knew that at the time, of course. We just stood and suffered while CBS television set up its cameras.

The Malibu event was the first race in which I realized that, in order to survive a triathlon, you must sometimes first survive the elements. That might sound a bit dramatic, but, in fact, staying alive in the water at Malibu came to be a very real concern for many of us.

I remember stopping about three-quarters of the way through the swim to catch my bearings and to see if my feet were still attached to my ankles—I'd lost feeling in my extremities some time before. Ten yards away from me, my brother Jeff was doing the same thing. He had a look of fear in his eyes that I'll never forget—as if we were hiking and had stumbled into an angry bear. Then we saw a lifeguard on a surfboard 50 yards away. "Do you guys want a ride in to shore?" the guard asked us. We both sprinted in his direction, but since Jeff was the faster swimmer and the board would hold only one passenger, I was forced to continue

**The start of the ill-fated Malibu Triathlon in 1982.
We don't think about wetsuits,
just the $14,000 in prize money.**

the race. Jeff was added to the 19 or so athletes who were pulled from the water and sent to the half-dozen hot showers made available at the last minute.

Not surprisingly, the two men who placed first and second at Malibu were ex-competitive swimmers. Their slight bit of extra bulk certainly helped them in the cold water, but since Malibu, ex-swimmers have dominated triathlons with warm-water swims, too. This despite the fact that more than half of today's active triathletes come from running backgrounds. Why? Is there something about a swimming background that makes it particularly easy for an athlete to switch to triathlon training?

I think so. A person usually begins a swimming career at an early age. It's not uncommon for an eight- or nine-year-old to be staring at the line on the bottom of a pool for three or four hours a day. And they aren't just making their little bodies stronger; they're developing their minds, dealing with the boredom of endurance training and learning the discipline required to develop fully their athletic potential. Usually, they have ready role models—older, faster swimmers in the same pool, just a lane or two over—and plenty of peer pressure to keep them motivated.

Like most other things, of course, experience can work both ways. A friend of mine, Charlie Graves, is a former All-American freestyler and one of the best swimmers on the national professional triathlon circuit. While he admits that the prodigious training he did as a kid—up to 20,000 yards a day—prepared him well for endurance sports, Charlie is, in his own words, "sick of swimming." He swims now only two or three days a week—just enough to maintain his base. Happily for Charlie, that's still enough to keep him right up in front of even the biggest triathlons.

As important as motivation and discipline, perhaps more so, the young swimmer develops a "feel" for the water. This is a rather nebulous concept, but it's a significant one, especially if you've learned to swim competitively late in the game and are trying unsuccessfully to keep up with someone with a long swimming background—despite the fact that you're doing more mileage and lifting heavier weights more often. A swimmer with a good feel for the water moves efficiently, making minute adjustments in his or her stroke without thinking, changing arm and hand positions constantly in an effort to find still water, to become perfectly aqua-dynamic. I've been swimming hard for five years now, and I've only just begun to develop "feel."

All is not lost for the late starter, of course. Two young triathletes I know, George Hoover and Chris Miller, both from Del Mar, California, became excellent swimmers in their late 20s with less than a year of formal training. Both, however, had strong backgrounds as surfers and paddlers, and they both received some excellent coaching on the way to the top. From the moment they entered the pool, there was someone walking alongside, making sure that they didn't fall into bad habits that would be hard to break later on.

Overcoming the Fear

For most runners or cyclists without swimming backgrounds, the swim portion of a triathlon is something to be afraid of, not simply to train for. It's this fear factor that makes the event seem so difficult. "I *know* I can ride a bike," they'll say, "and I know I can walk if I have to during the run, but I'd have trouble with the swim."

Admissions of fear about the swim are perhaps the most common apprehension voiced by budding triathletes. In one sense, that's strange, because a recent national poll put swimming on the top of the list of America's favorite recreational activities. (Cycling was second; running was a dismal eighth.)

Trying to get my shoes on at the Malibu Triathlon. Everyone's lips were blue and shaking; hands and arms were shivering too hard to tie laces or work snaps. With the rain, no one warmed up—even on the bike.

Consider, though, that most triathlon swims take place in open water and begin with chaotic mass starts in which a certain amount of kicking and clawing is inevitable (although the popularity of the age group wave start, first used in the Bud Light U.S. Triathlon Series in 1984, is changing this). Even the experts get nervous. The key is to swim enough to feel comfortable in the water—know your level of ability intimately. Mass swim starts are no places for egomaniacs. Second, try to combine all the proper elements of swim conditioning into a workable training program, then follow it. Confidence in your level of fitness can work wonders.

Learning How

Proper stroke technique is critical for both confidence and efficiency, so joining an organized program with a coach—a Masters swim team, for instance—is a big help. You can be in excellent cardiovascular shape and still have trouble moving through the water because you have a poor stroke. The coach can help you in ways in which it would be impossible to help yourself, regardless of how hard you train. If you can't find a coach, then at least make a trip to a bookstore and buy something that illustrates basic stroke mechanics. Knowing what is *supposed* to be happening is better than nothing.

A coach is important, too, in that he or she will monitor how you train, not just how much. Swimming lap after lap in the pool by yourself or mile after mile in the ocean or a lake might get you through a triathlon, but you'll reach top speed very quickly and stagnate. Group workouts with heavy emphasis on interval training are the only way to get faster. They're also the only way to cut through the most crushing obstacle to swim training: tedium. Personally, I cannot think of another physical activity as crushingly boring as going up and down a 25-yard pool time after time after time.

In any case, don't take your swimming lightly. If you're a beginning triathlete and you've been a swimmer in the past, don't assume that all you need to work on are two out of the three sports. You'll be rudely awakened in your first race— halfway to the turning buoy, when it's much too late. Confidence is important,

Wave starts by age group, first developed by the Bud Light USTS, are taking some of the kicking and clawing out of the mass start.

You're going to have to go in sooner or later.

yes, but it doesn't make up for good, solid work. A personal experience is a case in point:

When I first began swimming laps in 1975, I felt very comfortable in the water. Having grown up with a pool in the backyard and having surfed and sailed for years, I figured that there wouldn't be much to learning how to swim well. How wrong I was!

In college, I signed up for a Water Safety Instructor certification course to fulfill a PE requirement. The assignment for the first day of class was to swim 500 yards. No sweat, I thought. I had run some decent mile and two-mile times in high school, and even though I hadn't run much since then, I still was in pretty good shape. But not for swimming, I wasn't. I almost passed out getting through the 500, and it took me more than 12 minutes. I knew right then there was more to this swimming business than I had first assumed.

The best advice I can give you about swimming is to do the same. Assume the worst. Join a team or at least structure your workouts. Use a pool if possible to break up the boredom and get in some interval training. Build your confidence along with your upper body. Triathlons are tough enough without having to worry about drowning before the end of the first event.

SAMPLE WORKOUTS

Below are four sample workouts—actually, the same workout translated into four separate ability levels.

Unless you are an excellent swimmer with a national-class background like Charlie Graves, you probably need to swim at least five days a week. I swim six, mostly because I was never in Charlie's league, and just to stay close I've got to work my butt off.

The basic weekly structure that is popular with a lot of the athletes I train with—and the one I follow—is two hard days followed by an easy day, two hard days followed by a rest day, then one medium day.

What's hard, easy, or medium? You'll have to answer that one for yourself. If you're nervous about driving to your workout on Monday, then need someone to help you open the car door so you can drive home afterward, I guess that's hard. If you can *run* the 20 miles home after swimming on Wednesday, I suppose that's easy.

Keep in mind that swimming is gentle to your body. You might get a sore shoulder once in a while, but your body can handle much more stress in the pool than it could ever handle running or cycling. Take advantage of this: Eighty to 90 percent of your swim training should be in the form of intervals. Try that with running, and you'll end up in the hospital.

The four ability levels:

Level 1—The beginner with little or no swimming background

Level 2—The middle-of-the-pack triathlete trying to make the most of a heavy schedule

Level 3—The moderately successful competitor hoping to place well in his or her age division

Level 4—The professional or aspiring contender or the top age-grouper looking for rapid improvement

The key:

In the workouts listed below, "10 × 75 @ :30" means 10 75-yard (or meter) swims on a 30-second interval. An interval is the time you should take to complete the distance *and* rest. In this case, you would be pushing off the wall every 30 seconds to start the next swim within the set (one "set" would be four 75-yard swims, for example, at level 1).

Level 1

100-yard warm-up
4 × 75 @ 1:15
2 × 200 @ 4:00
200-yard pull

3 × 50 kick @ 1:30
3 × 100 @ 2:30
4 × 25 sprint @ :45

Total: 750 yards

Level 2

200-yard warm-up
6 × 75 @ 1:30
2 × 200 @ 3:30
2 × 300 pull w/1 min. rest
   between
4 × 50 @ 1:30
4 × 100 @ 2:00
100-yard cool-down

Total: 2,500 yards

Level 3

300-yard warm-up
8 × 75 @ 1:15
4 × 200 @ 3:00—break each at 150, take 5 sec. rest, then finish

2 × 400 pull w/1 min. rest between
6 × 50 @ 1:15
6 × 100 @ 1:45
8 × 25 sprint @ :30
200-yard cool-down

Total: 3,500 yards

Level 4

400-yard warm-up
10 × 75 @ 1:00
5 × 200 @ 2:30—break each at 150, take 5 sec. rest, then finish

2 × 500 pull w/:30 rest between
8 × 50 @ 1:45
10 × 100 @ 1:20
10 × 25 sprint @ :20
200-yard cool-down

Total: 5,000 yards

A FEW HINTS

Adapt the workouts to fit your individual hard/medium/easy day routine by changing the intervals in one or more of the sets.

Also, rather than concentrating on mileage, be consistent in your workouts and try to keep the quality of your training high. Challenge yourself on the hard days by trying to hold increasingly faster intervals. Remember, as opposed to running and cycling, your body is being supported on all sides when you're swimming. It can take hard workout after hard workout without physically breaking down.

Going for the Big Swim

Preparing for triathlons with open-water swims means swimming in open water beforehand—there's no getting around it. You'll encounter three problems, two of which you probably won't have to face in a pool:

Fear. If you're afraid in the pool, perhaps you'd better stick to biathlons. If you're afraid in the open water, you're one of many.

Swimming in the ocean or in large lakes is mostly a mental thing. How many times, for instance, during a thousand-yard swim in a pool, do you touch bottom?

Relaxation is the key. Breathe deeply before you begin an open-water swim to get the lungs working. Don't fight the waves or the chop; flow with them. In practice, become familiar with the feeling of swimming close to someone else in the open water. You won't have a choice in the race.

One word of warning, however: while fear is debilitating, overconfidence can be dangerous. A healthy respect for the ocean or large bodies of open water is important, as my experience at the Malibu Triathlon demonstrates. Cold water, big waves, currents, collisions with other swimmers, or disorientation on a poorly marked course can throw you off your stride.

I enjoy a story about a major, nationally ranked collegiate swim team taking a group vacation in Hawaii. They all decided that a romp in the big surf on the north shore of Oahu would be a treat. With years of training and world-class competition under their belts, but with no knowledge at all of wave action, rip currents, and undertow, they hit the beach. Several were literally saved from drowning by lifeguards who wouldn't have made the junior varsity team back at school, but who knew the ocean in general and the local area in particular.

The lesson the swimmers learned, of course, is one no triathlete should forget: training and ability in one environment doesn't always translate into success in another. Get into shape. Practice in the open water. A shortfall in either area will hurt your performance.

Navigation. There are no lane lines in the ocean. Pick out landmarks before you begin and sight on them as you go. Practice swimming with your head out of the water—it's tougher than it looks. Also, practice guiding on other swimmers. Letting someone else do all the head-up swimming is a great way to save energy.

Hypothermia. There are times when the water will be cold enough that hypothermia is unavoidable—when your body's core temperature is going to fall no matter what you wear or how fast you swim. My advice in that case is very simple: don't swim.

Long before that point, though, there are precautions you can take that will help you deal with water in the mid- to low 60s. When the water dips far below that—below 58 or 59, say—you're getting beyond the range of mass participation triathlons.

**Practice in the open water.
Learn to navigate.**

**When the water dips into
the low 60s or even lower,
hypothermia is a
possibility. Wear a wetsuit
if you're in doubt as to
your ability to handle the
cold, then swim like crazy.**

First, practice. Your body will acclimatize to cold water over a period of time. Some triathletes have been known even to work up to cold swimming by standing in cold showers, although any adjustment there, I'm sure, is purely mental. Repeated ocean or lake swims interspersed with your pool workouts during triathlon season will get you used to water on the low end of the thermometer.

Second, when in doubt, use a wet suit. They are legal in most triathlons because the added buoyancy is negated by the fact that they make you a lot slower. Whether you wear a full suit or a vest depends on the conditions. Wet suits are discussed further in Chapter 9.

If, despite everything, you do get caught in a tough situation, don't be afraid to call for help. In fact, make up your mind before a cold swim to do just that, because hypothermia can make your brain work like a clock with honey in the works. Numb fingers and toes are the first signs. If you get to the point where the arms and legs aren't working, and you begin to lose your sense of orientation, call it quits.

"You'd better step on it; he's catching us."

"He's still catching us."

"Ahh, pick it up please, he's still catching us."

"Wow, pull over; let him go by. How fast are we going?"

"Fifty-one? Jeez, he went by us like a shot."—Mike Plant to the press truck driver at the Denver Bud Light USTS as Scott Molina passed them on a long downhill during the cycling portion of the race.

4
CYCLING

I'd do it differently today—I'd take better advantage of the opportunity it presented—but I knew just what to say when Jim Lampley of ABC's "Wide World of Sports" asked me the question at the finish line of the February 1982 Ironman. I was tired and irritable, despite having just won the biggest triathlon in the world, and I wanted to be with my wife, Virginia. Lampley, on the other hand, wanted to talk. "Scott," he asked, "what was the difference between your race today and last year?" (I'd placed third in 1981, behind John Howard and Tom Warren.)

He pointed his microphone in my direction, and I answered quickly, without really thinking. I was truthful, but a little blunt, perhaps even sarcastic. It had been a long day. "I learned how to ride a bike," I replied, then headed in the other direction. End of interview.

Well, a win at the Ironman and an interview on ABC television seem a lot more important now than they did then. But if I had another chance to answer that question today—in seven words or less—I couldn't be more accurate. Learning how to ride a bike is what makes runners and swimmers into triathletes—fair triathletes into good ones, good ones into stars.

Understand here what I mean when I say "learn." While the bicycle is not as common a mode of transportation in this country as in some countries in Europe or the Far East, the bike in an American garage is a little like soy sauce in the refrigerator. Even if you never use it, it's there. For a kid in California or Nebraska or Massachusetts, learning how to ride a "two-wheeler" is part of the experience of growing up.

On the other hand, relatively few Americans actually participate in organized

37

John Howard taught everyone
how important cycling could be
in a triathlon.

cycling, and far fewer have ever raced bicycles. The technical considerations of
proper fit, gear ratios, RPMs, aerodynamic body position, and frame configura-
tion are as alien to most people in this country as the cockpit of the space shuttle.
Few people have "learned" how to ride a bike in any way that will help them do
more than get to the beach and back. But, as a triathlete, you *need* to know more
than that if you ever want to go beyond simple survival toward some kind of
gradual improvement.

In 1981, John Howard showed me and the rest of the young triathlon
community how important it is to understand our bikes. For years the premier
road cyclist in this country, Howard had come to the Ironman in 1980 with
almost no preparation in swimming or running, but still finished third. Then he
returned the next year, somehow kept himself from drowning in Kailua Bay, then
got on his bike and dusted everyone in the field. Fully equipped with a state-of-
the-art machine and tight-fitting racing outfit, low to his handlebars with his
arms bent and his long fingers draped over his brake hoods, he went by me as if
I were standing still. It was a rude awakening, especially since I thought I was
well prepared with a $250, 25-inch SR Gran Course, $8 cleated shoes, and a neat
little tool kit beneath the seat with vise-grip pliers inside just in case.

Howard was one of the few competitive cyclists to make the jump into the
triathlon (few have even as of now), but the sport was never the same after his
arrival. He showed us that minutes—sometimes tens of minutes—could be
shaved off finishing times by riding a good bike well. Even better, the total
energy expended might in some situations be even less than had been simply
wasted by pedaling a 40-pound monster around for 20 or 30 miles or more.

Although he wasn't conscious of his role at the time (he was, after all, merely
doing what he'd been doing better than any other American for years and years),
John Howard moved the sport of triathlon away from the philosophy of grind-

it-out-and-survive-against-all-odds and toward a realization that technical considerations are critical.

Most technical considerations in a triathlon have to do with cycling. Training programs in swimming and running can get complicated, but they don't have to be. (The best ones, to me, are the ones that aren't.) In cycling, though, what you are able to accomplish is related directly to what kind of machine you're sitting on—and how familiar you are with it. You have to deal with chains and gears and sprockets, tires that blow, wheels that wobble.

There are several reasons why it's important for you, as a triathlete, to become a knowledgeable cyclist. First, what you *don't* know can hurt your performance. Frames that aren't the right size, seats or handlebars that are too high can lead to fatigue, soreness, and even injury.

Second, knowing how to handle your bike can keep you out of trouble. Quite simply, racing a bicycle can be dangerous business. Spending a lot of time in your seat, becoming a better bike handler simply by becoming familiar with the equipment, can help you recognize and avoid hazardous competitive situations.

Third, and perhaps most important, since cycling is the pivotal event in most triathlons, your ability as a cyclist has a tremendous amount to do with your overall success in a race. Simple. But there's more to it than just that.

Perhaps nothing has been as important to my success in the sport as being able to ride hard in a race, then come off the bike and *run* hard. There are plenty of good runners in the sport, and a lot of good riders, too, but in the end it's the triathletes who can put the two sports together who win races and continue to improve—and that's not something that often comes naturally. It takes work and time. You have to be able to ride the bike hard and well, but also efficiently, with a knowledge of both your limitations and those of your machine.

Aerodynamics are more critical on the bike than in any other stage of a triathlon.

GETTING STARTED

The Novice Cyclist

First the good news: as a swimmer or a runner, you'll probably improve as a triathlete a lot more than if you were a cyclist trying to become a swimmer or a runner. There's not the fear of open water to overcome or the high levels of fatigue that most beginning runners have to face.

Now the bad news: the key to improvement on the bike is putting in the effort, which brings you flat up against the nemesis of triathletes everywhere—the time factor. To get better, you need to spend time in the saddle. There's no way around it. You can go out and get a good workout in the pool in 45 minutes. You can run hard for half an hour and get your heart rate up high and be satisfied. But as a cyclist, especially in the beginning, you need to be able to go out and *gradually* get used to sitting in the seat for a couple of hours at a time, minimum. That doesn't mean that a hard workout of an hour or even less on the bike isn't valuable—and we'll talk about that later in this chapter—but simply sitting and pedaling at a moderate rate, perhaps doing nothing more than concentrating on form and enjoying the scenery, is about the best thing a novice cyclist can do.

As a triathlete with a running background, I was lucky to be in a situation where building a good, strong base of mileage on the bike came very naturally. I came in on the ground floor—the sport was growing as I did—so I was able to build slowly, without pressure. Fifty miles a week was a lot at one time—state of the art. Then 100 miles a week was enough, then 200 or 300, until now, there are times when I'll put in 500 miles a week. The temptation for a beginner in 1985 is to jump right in and go for the big miles all at once. Avoid it. All you're likely to achieve is an injury.

The First Step: Buy the Right Equipment. There are plenty of experts in the field and plenty of books on the subject, so all I'm going to do here is give you three simple rules:

Rule 1: Buy a bike that fits you. The best way to do this is go to a reputable bike shop near where you live and ask a lot of questions. A general rule of thumb is that you should be able to straddle the top tube of the bike with your feet flat on the floor and have one inch of clearance between your crotch and the top tube. But it's more complicated than that. Fitting a bike takes dozens of considerations into account, and adjustments that may relieve or cause a knee injury or a stiff back can be as fine as a millimeter or two. There are expert mechanics or cyclists who might charge as much as $100 just to "set you up" on a piece of equipment. Buy a book to become familiar with the terminology, then head for the shop.

Rule 2: Buy a bike that you can afford—and don't buy more than you need. The first part of Rule 2 is obvious. The second part is what makes triathletes very popular in bike shops—they tend to buy the best, even when the best is better than any of the professional riders competing in the Tour de France will ever need.

Mark Allen, looking lean and fit, on his way to winning the US Olympians Triathlon in Las Vegas in 1984. Keep the pedals spinning on the bike and the elbows bent to absorb shock.

Remember that cost—high or low—is not the only consideration. It's possible to walk into a shop and ask for the best and walk out with a $5,000 titanium-alloy-frame, fixed-gear track bike without brakes. What you do then is take it home and hang it on the wall and buy another bike you can use in triathlons.

"Knowledge and experience are hard won and not easily bought," says Bill Bryant, a top mechanic and former category 1 cyclist from the San Francisco area who served as the Team J David bike mechanic at the October 1982 Ironman. "A cyclist who has spent the time to be properly fitted to a medium-priced bike will be faster than the impatient novice who spent $1,700 on Italy's latest fantasy cycle and has ignored the necessary fitting nuances."

John Howard, who was my triathlete teammate in 1983, agrees. "I see a lot of beginners trying to compete at high speeds while being positioned poorly on a bike, using improper, faulty equipment on a bike that isn't set up correctly for them. Bicyclists have learned that the quickest, lightest, fastest bike is not always the best for a triathlon. Avoid high-priced gimmicks."

Rule 3: Make sure the quality of your bike doesn't hinder your competitiveness. This means that you should choose a middle ground between quality and practicality. Don't overspend, but don't scrimp, either. At the Ironman in 1981 I could have shaved maybe ten minutes off my time had I been on a better bike. That would have put me in second place.

Simply, find a bike that's in line with your ability level. There are hundreds out there to choose from. Get it fitted properly, then go to work.

Technique Counts for a Lot. Style on the bike is much more important than in running or even swimming. There have been many, many top distance runners over the years who looked like they were about to die along the way to setting world records. And while the "feel" for the water we talked about in the preceding chapter is important, there is plenty of room for individuality in open-water stroke mechanics.

Group rides can make long rides bearable. One way or another you'll need to build mileage on the bike to improve.

In cycling, on the other hand, streamlining yourself is critical because your major enemy is wind resistance. Some experts say that simply pushing the air in front of you accounts for 40 percent of your energy on a bike. And the faster you go, the worse it gets. Being comfortable is important, too. Preventing fatigue in long races where you're going to have to bounce off the bike and run is critical.

The very best way to become a better technical cyclist is to ride with people who are better than you are. Sounds easy, but if you come from a running or a swimming background, you may be surprised at how hard it is to find competitive cyclists willing to help.

I'm not really sure why that last statement is true. It *sounds* silly, but plenty of novice competitive cyclists have found it to be so. Perhaps it is the fact that cycling *is* so technical—that it takes so long to work your way through the ranks—that neither those who are on the way up nor those who have made it are anxious to share what got them there. Perhaps it is the highly structured competitive format of the sport—the categories and the licenses and the clothing regulations. Whatever, the undercurrent of elitism that pervades competitive cycling is something that you'll probably bump up against. Stay with it; riding with people who have been riding for years and years will pay big dividends.

The best way I know to ensure yourself a regular, knowledgeable partner is to hire a coach. Better yet, share the coach (and the cost) by putting together a small group and riding together one or two days a week. There's so much knowledge about cycling to collect, so many tidbits of advice that can make a real difference in your performance, that working totally on your own is an exercise in frustration. And it can be counterproductive, too, because improper technique will be ingrained and hard to change when the error is pointed out later.

When first confronted by a real technical expert, even "experienced" triathletes are usually amazed at how much there is to learn about riding efficiently. To give you an idea, my brother Jeff, who finished third at the Ironman twice, was riding in San Diego one day when a cyclist came up behind him. "You must be a triathlete," the guy said. "Well, yeah, I am," said Jeff. "How did you know?" The cyclist laughed and shook his head. "I can tell by the way you ride," he said.

Listen to the tips your coach or an acknowledged expert has to offer, but perhaps even more important, *watch*. Try to translate what is said into the way it should look and the way it feels. Many things that feel awkward at first feel that way because you've been doing things wrong for so long.

Group rides are important in helping you improve. The miles fly by when you've got someone to talk to, so the time you must spend in the saddle is a lot easier to take. And even without a coach, the information that flows back and forth will keep your mind on the basic goal: getting better. For instance, you'll notice so-and-so riding with stiff arms, remember that that can lead to fatigue, and then notice how straight and stiff your own arms are. Or you might watch another rider beat everyone else to the top of a big hill, then mimic his or her technique on the next climb. It might work, it might not; can't hurt to try.

Spinning. The most common error novice cyclists make is simply pushing hard on the pedals and ignoring the upstroke—the pulling part of the pedal stroke—completely. "Plunging," as it is often called, is what my brother Jeff was doing when the unknown cyclist teased him on the road.

The need to use the entire pedal stroke is why cleats were developed. With your feet strapped to the pedals through the use of cleats, straps, and toe clips, you can pull up and still keep your shoe attached to the pedal. This allows you to use the back of your legs—the hamstrings and the calves—along with the large muscles of your thighs—the quadriceps— that are used to push down. Think about lifting your knees alternately and turning circles (spinning) with your feet. Forget pushing down completely until spinning becomes second nature. Ride frequently in low gears (big sprockets) so the temptation to push down on the pedals will be minimized. You'll turn more RPMs with your feet, and the spinning motion will be easier to feel. If your butt bounces up and down on the seat when you're pedaling at high RPMs, it's a good sign that you are still putting more emphasis on pushing down than on pedaling around.

The best way I found to develop my spinning technique is through regular use of an indoor trainer, or wind simulator. I *hate* training this way—it's about the most boring thing you can do—but I can't deny that it pays off in several areas. Simply, a wind simulator is a stand for your bike that allows your rear tire to spin a small fan, which in turn pushes air and creates resistance similar to what you'd feel if you were out on the road. Set up a mirror in front of your trainer to check out your style, then listen to the sound of the fan fluctuate as you pedal. At first, you'll hear the sound vary in intensity because you're pushing down more than pulling up. When the sound of the fan is consistent through your entire pedal stroke, you know you're on the right track.

Another good technique to use on the trainer is to pedal with one foot. Some trainers even have a stationary attachment that allows you to clip your nonworking foot tight. In terms of conditioning, there's probably no tougher workout than 15 minutes with one foot on your Turbo-Trainer. And the ache in the hamstrings will tell even the most confident cyclist that there's a long way to go until the art of spinning is truly mastered.

Body Position and Comfort. Styles, of course, vary from cyclist to cyclist, with aerodynamics and comfort being prime considerations. Some general hints: keep your arms bent at all times to absorb shock, your knees and your elbows in, your shoulders down, and your head up. Again, a local expert is the best source of specific information—next to your own body, of course. If your back aches consistently after riding, or your knees or your neck are stiff and sore, some physical adjustments to the bike itself may be in order. Adjustments of less than an inch in saddle or handlebar stem height can make big differences in your performance, especially where running after cycling is concerned.

Scott Molina.

Experienced Cyclists

A relative few experienced cyclists will join the sport of triathlon, which is not to say they won't succeed. Guys like John Howard and Marc Thompson, of Sherman, Texas, a former U.S. National Cycling Team member who finished fourth in the '83 Ironman, are evidence of that.

Experienced cyclists have one advantage in triathlons by virtue of the fact that many races—especially the long ones like the Ironman—are weighted in the cyclists' favor. Swimmers have dominated since the beginning, but that is largely because they've gone out and learned how to ride. And any edge that strong runners have is quickly negated by the beating their legs take before they get to the run.

As with so much in this sport, the major hurdles a good cyclist will have to overcome are mental ones. Better swimmers will invariably be out ahead of you, so riding hard in a catch-up mode will be a fact of life. But how hard do you go? *Too* hard will mean that better runners will be in a position to run you down during the last event.

The best strategy is to train hard in the other two sports, concentrating on balancing your abilities. Resist the temptation in competition to blow the field away on the bike and rely instead on your cycling experience to be more efficient. Remember, the first step in a noncyclist's improvement as a triathlete lies in his or her learning to ride a bike well. The second is getting strong enough on the bike to be able to run hard after riding. You've already got those cards in your pocket.

Most importantly, be patient when you begin a running program. Your aerobic conditioning from cycling will carry over, but the biomechanical demands of running will take some adjusting to.

"A cyclist's legs are real 'soft,' " warns Howard. "Running is a jarring sport. Cycling doesn't damage tendons and ligaments the way running does—you're just not ready for the pounding.

"It took me six months to adjust, with half of that being recovery periods from injuries—I was just hurt all the time. I was in good cardiovascular shape and went into the sport with a lot of enthusiasm. I tried to equal my cycling threshold on foot. It just burned me out."

THE TRAINING PROGRAM

Because cycling takes so much time, I work everything else around my biking. There are traffic considerations, environmental conditions, and, most of all, you have to have *light*. I don't go indoors on a wind simulator unless I absolutely have to. For that reason alone, regardless of anything else, I'm glad I live in southern California where it hardly ever rains and it's never too cold for a bike ride.

I've found mornings to be the best for cycling. The traffic is light, and it's easy to get up even on mornings when you're not feeling 100 percent, have a light

breakfast, and go. Running first is a lot tougher; muscles are tight, and you can't warm up quite as gradually as you can on a bike, so the injury potential is much greater.

If you're really pressed for time, commuting back and forth to work on your bike is a great way to get in the mileage. As a matter of fact, commuting by bike even if you get in a real workout is a good idea, especially for the beginner, since your main goal is to get comfortable on the machine by simply sitting in the saddle as much as possible. A fairly reliable rule of thumb: in average traffic, you can go just about half as fast on a bike as you can in a car.

As with running, don't depend on the same ride, day after day, to keep you in top condition. Do so, and you'll reach a peak very early in your training and stay there. Long rides, rest days, and speed work all should be worked into every training week, although you'll find that, as in swimming, you'll gradually be able to handle more and harder workouts closer together without fear of injury than you will in running.

The Long Ride

With experienced cyclists or triathletes, the 100-miler is the classic long ride. How long yours will be will depend on your individual program and goals, but extending your maximum distance by riding with a group of friends at a moderate pace will pay many dividends. Strength and endurance are critical for the triathlete, and you're going to have to run in competition when you come off the bike, so merely building to your competition distance won't be enough. Plan on your weekly long ride (almost by neccessity on a Saturday or Sunday), taking three to four hours at first, then building gradually to five or six.

Eating during the long ride is important. The term *bonking* refers to the light-headed, weak-kneed feeling you get when your body runs out of fuel in the middle of a ride. Avoid it by eating a healthy breakfast before you hit the road and by carrying along a snack and a couple of water bottles. Bring money, too, for a lunch break and for emergencies.

Speed Work

I don't do much speed training on the bike by the clock. There's too much enjoyment in riding to different areas with a small group and playing competitive games along the way. In San Diego, our long, hard rides on Wednesday have become famous both for their social aspect and for the tremendous workout they provide. The group gets up to 25 or 30 people when everyone is in town; we ride up the coast from Del Mar (just north of La Jolla) to Dana Point—about 50 miles. Going north, we pick up riders along the way and ride at a leisurely pace, trading stories and gossip and picking up tips from the competitive cyclists who started to join the rides in late '84. Then we put the hammer down heading south: we sprint for city limit signs, sprint up hills, test each other by doing sudden "jumps" away from the pack. It's highly competitive—we drop people off the back of the pack the entire way south—but it's fun, too, even for the athletes who can't keep up, because each week they get closer and stay longer.

Hill Climbing

Hill climbing is an excellent form of speed and strength training that can be incorporated into almost every workout (unless, of course, you live in a part of the country where there aren't any hills). Coming out of the saddle on short, steep upgrades will help you build anaerobic potential; staying in the saddle on long, gradual grades builds strength. Use both techniques so that you are comfortable with them, keeping in mind that your size and weight will determine which position is more efficient for you. Small, light cyclists are usually better out of the saddle; a larger cyclist usually does better sitting down. In any case, be careful about trying to push too hard a gear when you're climbing; that's the most common cause of knee injuries to cyclists. ("High" gears are those in which your chain is on the smaller rear sprockets. They are harder to pedal.) Also, remember to use the entire pedal stroke—turn circles with your pedals instead of just pushing down. One top cyclist in the San Diego area recommends that,

while climbing hills sitting in the saddle, you keep your feet flat and imagine lifting a concrete construction block up toward your knee with your instep.

Time-Trialing

In competitive cycling, a time trial is a race where cyclists start at timed intervals and ride the course alone. No drafting is allowed, and the winner is the rider with the fastest time over the course. In a road race, everyone starts together, drafting and team strategy are critical elements, and the winner is the first athlete across the line.

Generally, time-trialing is the method used in most triathlons, but an informal time trial can also be an important part of your training routine. Ride a set course every week or two and keep your eye on the clock. Ride hard, and to simulate race conditions as closely as possible, ride with a friend who is close to you in ability. You'll push each other harder than you'd be able to push yourself alone. Keep a record of your progress week to week. You'll be amazed at how quickly you'll improve.

BIKE SAFETY

The 1982 Nice (France) Triathlon was one of the first races that challenged triathletes with a technically difficult bike course. The French, with their strong national background in cycling, gave us a route through the foothills of the Alps on which you could gain, or lose, a lot of time, not only on the uphills, but especially on the long, twisting downhills. It all depended on your bike-handling ability.

I've always enjoyed the Nice event, but I've always had trouble there. In '82 and again in '83, I crashed a week before the race. The first year, I had had a front tire blow on a downhill at the Malibu Triathlon and was still recovering from a broken collarbone. In '83 I took a nasty fall while training on the Nice course itself, so I went into the race feeling tentative about attacking the hills— something I knew I needed to do, since I was competing against Mark Allen, Dave Scott, and Scott Molina, who are all terrific swimmers.

That year on the bike, Allen and Molina were ahead, and I had just caught Dave near the top of the long climb through the mountains. Then I missed a turn and rode a quarter-mile or so before I realized what I'd done, so I had to do a U-turn and chase him all over again. By now I was in fifth; Ferdy Massimino, a physician from northern California who had placed 10th in the Ironman in October '82, had gone by me, too. A little bit up the road Ferdy missed a turn *completely*, crashed into a wall, and hurt himself pretty badly.

Finally, at the very top, I took a fast, 180-degree turn a little wide and bounced off a car moving in the opposite direction. I didn't crash, but instead of being psyched to go down this terrible hill, I was scared to death. People were falling all around me! I lost a lot of time on that downhill.

Safety when you're racing on a bike is a relative thing; you have to weigh the risks. If you're competing seriously, then you might decide to race harder than you think you should. You might fall, or burn yourself out (*blowing up* is the term a lot of endurance athletes use), but, on the other hand, you might pick up a couple of minutes. I *always* have to race like that, since I'm usually behind coming out of the swim.

The important thing is to know what your capabilities are, then be confident in your ability to maximize them. I've talked to Greg Lemond and Jonathan Boyer about fear, and they tell me that they psych themselves up *not* to be scared in a competitive situation. As soon as you become fearful, they say, the danger factor increases dramatically. You tighten up through turns and make mistakes through momentary indecision. You *think* rather than act, and that's when you get yourself in trouble.

Protect Yourself

The best way to eliminate the fear factor is to take practical precautions. Influenced by the Europeans, most of us rode that bike course in Nice without helmets, but I'd never ride it again without one.

Wear gloves, because if you go down, they'll prevent a lot of wear and tear on your hands. Also, make sure your tires are in good condition. If you're using sew-ups, make sure they're glued well. Check any type of tire for glass or defects and make sure there's plenty of tread so the tire will hold the road well through tight turns. Having a front tire blow or roll off a rim on a downhill curve is much more than an inconvenience—it can kill you.

Generally, keep your bike in good condition. Even if a poorly maintained machine stays together, just knowing that it *might* give you trouble is enough to make you back off—and, as I said, that's the *worst* situation to be in. You need to be relaxed and confident in your ability to go as fast as your bike will take you.

Crashing

Everyone who trains and races on a bike goes down. According to John Howard, there are only two kinds of bike riders in the world: those who have fallen and those who are going to fall. That isn't encouraging news, but there it is.

Take the precautions mentioned above to minimize the effects and don't dwell on the prospects. Do, however, stay out of obviously dangerous situations. When you're racing in a triathlon, give the other riders as wide a berth as possible. Wear a helmet even when it's not required. Give parked cars with people sitting on the driver's side wide berth, because suddenly opened car doors are a major cause of cycling injuries. Ride on roads full of traffic confidently, as if you belong there. Being tentative will force you into no-win situations.

When crashes happen, they happen quickly. The first time you go down hard, it's a real shock. My first bad fall came in Malibu, when a front tire blew on a 40 mph downhill, and I didn't quite believe what had happened until after I got up and brushed myself off. If you feel yourself going, relax and don't fight it. Cover your head with your arms if possible. Better to limit the damage to scrapes and bruises (*road rash* is the term) than to suffer a broken bone that will take you off the road completely.

DEALING WITH THE WEATHER

The ideal training ground for a cyclist, of course, is a place like southern California, where it may get cool but never cold, and where rain is relatively rare. When riding in cool or cold weather, the obvious additions to your wardrobe are called for: tights, gloves, earmuffs on your hat, etc. Cycling clothing manufacturers are getting more creative every year, and it would be silly to go into depth on the clothing issue. (I do talk more about it in Chapter 9.) In general, wear multiple layers of light- or medium-weight clothing that can be peeled off as you warm up. Beware, however, of peeling off so much that your sweaty body chills; hypothermia on the bike is a danger, especially when the temperature is low and the humidity is high.

The alternative that comes in a distant second even to cold-weather riding outdoors is the indoor trainer. Many varieties recently have been introduced to the market, so I'd recommend you head for the bike shop and ask for an explanation.

On the plus side, indoor trainers are the only way to get a good cycling workout when it's dark or the weather's bad. I've already mentioned that they're also a great way to sharpen your technique. The terrible part about them is the crushing boredom of pedaling along for hours without a change in scenery.

A friend of mine who lives in the East told me about how he and his wife used to go down into their basement, turn off all the lights, turn on the heater, and sit on their indoor trainers for two hours. "Didn't that just fry your mind?" I asked him.

"Yeah," he said. "We could only do it about once a week, but it was awesome. We'd turn the light on, and there'd be this big pool of sweat. . . ."

Another guy I know puts a bike with an impossibly difficult fixed gear on his trainer and pedals away. He knows when he's finished—when the pool of sweat flows to a certain point in the room.

In any case, the trainers are at least better than rollers, which existed long before the wind simulators came along. The rollers are tough to use because you have to balance your bike on them and pedal, then have someone or something to grab when you stop. I was using a roller machine one time at home and wasn't watching what I was doing. I moved to the right side of the rollers and then the bike came off. My wheels were still spinning like crazy, of course, and I rode into the television set I was watching at about 25 miles an hour—just blew the whole thing apart.

I'll take a long, cool ride on a January day in San Diego any time.

"You count every mile and every aid station. You think, 'When is this gonna end?' Four hours of running. Can you believe that? Six hours of biking and four hours of running. That's insane!"—Julie Leach after her win at the October '82 Ironman

5
ON THE RUN

Most of the best triathletes in the world are former swimmers. Dave Scott, Scott Molina, Mark Allen, Mark Suprenant, and many others all did well in the pool in age group, high school, and college competition. No one has been able to come up with the exact reason why this is so, but the most widely accepted theory is that they adapted well to the sport of triathlon because they spent years putting in lap after lap, mile after mile, in water, preparing themselves not only physically, but mentally as well, for the long hours of triathlon training.

I go along with that theory. The fact is, though, that most triathletes within the ranks—the good, the average, the back-of-the-packer—began as runners. Some grew bored after they had done what they set out to do in the marathon or after their 10K times began to stagnate. Some moved into multisport events as an offshoot of training they did to supplement their running while injured. Others simply began to see their bodies and their levels of fitness in a different light.

The physical ideal for most endurance athletes at the peak of the running boom during the mid-1970s was a pair of strong legs beneath as little else as possible. Emaciation was in; muscles were out. But as the concept of general fitness began to take hold, many runners began to wonder where their upper bodies had disappeared to. Their pride in the look of the malnourished began to fade as their friends who had taken up swimming or weightlifting began to sprout real arms and shoulders. For reasons of injury prevention, aesthetics, and overall health, it became obvious that running required supplemental training of one kind or another. The sport of triathlon, loaded with incentive and prestige, offered a perfect solution.

Still, running remains the basis of many triathletes' fitness programs, mostly because it is the simplest and purest of the three sports of the triathlon. You don't need a machine or an ocean; you don't need a dry road or even a warm one. Sometimes you don't even need shoes. Running will always be closest to my heart because, like so many of you, I began as a runner. I owe much of my early success in this sport to my running ability. Given the choice, I will always run.

I started running in high school, mostly by accident. Dreaming of touchdowns and dates with cheerleaders, I went out for football as a freshman, although about all I accomplished with my five-foot, three-inch, 130-pound body was to get bounced around. The required off-season weightlifting program probably would have helped, but I was excused that first year because I'd injured my back on the trampoline. (I put my head through the springs trying to do something ridiculous. Hurting my back was no problem—I was lucky I didn't lose my ears.) The coach wasn't about to let me off entirely, though. "Tinley," he said, "if you can't lift, then you'll run. There's the track. Start running. Don't stop until I come get you."

So I ran. At first I went a quarter of the way around the quarter-mile track, then walked, then I ran another quarter and so on. By the end of the semester, I could run five miles without stopping, which did a lot for my sense of personal accomplishment. It didn't do a thing for my confidence in ever being able to be a football star. All I could think about were those guys getting big and strong and mean back in the weight room.

The next spring I tried out for the baseball team and got cut, so I decided to go out for track. After all, I at least had some experience in plodding along for extended periods of time, courtesy of the football coach. As it turned out, though, I'd been doing more than plodding. The distance runners had been training for over a week that first day I showed up, but I was surprised (and *they* were surprised) by how easily I could keep up. At running, it seemed, I was a natural. I'd found a niche.

Distance running in high school was a lot of work, but I was attracted to it because I didn't have to rely on other team members to show up; I had no excuses when something went wrong. It was my mistake and not the fact that somebody dropped the ball or ran the wrong way or something. The pure simplicity of the sport was intriguing to me then and now—even in the midst of constant triathlon training. It's easy to lose perspective sometimes, to become wrapped up in obligations and schedules and week after week of competition. But an early morning 10-mile cross-country run by myself can still take me away from all of that when nothing else can. The pure simplicity of running is the sport's most valuable commodity.

GETTING STARTED

There are three groups of beginners in the sport of triathlon: (1) the absolute rookie with little or no experience in any of the three sports; (2) the athlete with a background in running, but little in one or both of the other two; (3) the experienced cyclist or swimmer with little or no running background. Each type of triathlete is faced with his or her own set of problems, and each has an advantage or two over the other. One problem they all face is doing too much too soon. After all, isn't a triathlon—that infamously cruel test of survival—the ultimate goal? Isn't overdoing everything the ultimate challenge?

Wrong and wrong. There are triathlons that are tests of survival and some that aren't. *Most* aren't. And they should never be cruel. Pushing yourself beyond acceptable limits is never a good policy. Training intelligently, building a base slowly, then easing into a competitive framework will keep you from burning out, both physically and mentally.

The Beginner

The scope of this book is not sufficient to provide the absolute novice with enough information to begin a comprehensive running program. There are some very good books in the field whose sole aim is in that direction, and I'd recommend running (literally) out to the bookstore and picking one up. Then walk home. (They're all going to tell you to start slowly.) Two that are especially good are the late Jim Fixx's *Complete Book of Running* and Jeff Galloway's *Galloway's Book on Running*. Fixx's book was a landmark when it was first published in 1977, and it remains at the top of my list today. Galloway's work is more technical—it leans toward charts and plans and strategies, but Galloway's way to improvement is through enjoyable, injury-free running and is particularly applicable to the triathlete.

Up the first big hill at the Ironman—running off the bike is the first challenge of the novice triathlete.

The Experienced Runner

If you've never run after a hard bike ride, you're in for a surprise. I've known first-time triathletes to jump off their bikes, run a few steps, then stare down in amazement at their legs, which *look* familiar but feel like they belong to the old man on the beach cruiser they passed four miles down the road.

The swim and the bike portions of a triathlon (and since most triathlons have adopted the swim/bike/run format, just assume that order unless I warn you first) are the great equalizers. Top runners have come into this sport expecting instant greatness, only to find that much less talented but more experienced triathletes can run away from them with ease after an hour or two of hard biking.

In 1984, at the Bud Light USTS National Championship in Bass Lake, California, I was blown away on the run by a guy I'd never seen before. I was surprised, to say the least, because at that point the only triathletes I thought were capable of that—and then only on occasion—were Scott Molina, Mark Allen, and Dave Scott. It turned out that the mystery man was Curtis Alitz, who swam and ran competitively for the U.S. Military Academy at West Point and in 1978 placed fourth in the NCAA Championships in the 10,000-meter run with a 28:46. It was impressive that Curt had been able to stay close to the lead on the hilly Bass Lake bike course, but even more impressive that he still had enough in his legs to run as well as he did afterward. It was an exception to the rule, but as with most rules, you can break them only so many times. At the '84 Ironman a month later he had a good swim and a fair bike, but his marathon was an ordeal—it took him over 4 hours and 20 minutes.

If you're a triathlete with a running background, the biggest obstacle in your path is probably going to be you. The first time out on a run after a hard bike ride, you'll expect to be able to run up to your ability levels. When you don't (and you probably won't even come close), don't be surprised. In fact, it's best not to even *try* to run too hard in competition or during workouts until you've gotten a good deal of training under your belt and until you've raced frequently enough to give your legs a chance to adjust to the new bike/run demands. Patience, in this case, is more than a virtue—it's a necessity.

I had a little advantage when I started out because the early triathlons I did were short and the order was all screwed up. In some of them the run was *first*. Then there were some where the run was last, and a lot of them were the run/swim/bike/swim/run things in San Diego. I had four years of gradual exposure to having to run after having ridden a bike.

In the '81 Ironman I had my first experience with having to do a full run after having really thrashed my legs on the bike. I had done several half-Ironman-distance races before that, but for the most part I never really rode that hard, mostly because my ability level hadn't been that high. I came off the bike at Ironman in 18th or 19th place and just started running with no expectations. I felt *terrible*, but I kept feeling better and better, and everyone else kept feeling worse and worse. Even though I was running slowly, at least I was running. A lot of people weren't even doing that. I passed 15 guys, ran a 3:21 marathon, and ended up third. I'm sure that having more experience than most in running after riding, or even running after doing *anything* in competition, even if it was just for fun, helped quite a bit.

The next year, in February 1982, when I won the Ironman, going into the run knowing that I could handle the marathon was a big psychological advantage. Sometimes that's all you need. There are few times when running after biking is going to feel *great*, but if you know that eventually your legs are going to come back to you—say, in a mile or two—then you can afford to be patient. Confidence counts for a lot.

If you've come into triathlons with a good background in running, be assured that the base you've built will eventually begin to work for you. At first, however, be prepared to watch your running performance suffer. That will happen for several reasons.

To begin with, you'll be putting in less mileage as you start to train in the other two sports. That's a good thing in that you'll probably suffer fewer running-related injuries, but a tough thing to adjust to mentally. Top marathoners regularly train 100 miles per week, with buildups to 120 and beyond in preparation for a major race. Top triathletes run less than half that. If you've been running 60–80 miles per week, you'll be able to get by with 30–40 as a triathlete. The problem comes in telling yourself to relax and not worry that all the mileage you put in when you were just running is going down the drain. It's not.

The pure simplicity of running is its most valuable attribute.

Individually, where your specific mileage will fall is up to your program and goals you decide are best for you. More about that in Chapter 6.

Your running will initially suffer also because your body is adapting to the stresses of cycling and swimming. You might think that your arms and upper body have little to do with your being able to run well, but that's far from the truth. Prove it by swimming right after a hard run or vice versa. Stiff? Tight? Your arms feel like lead? You're not alone.

The process of becoming a triathlete who is strong in all three sports is a very gradual one that can't be pushed. Talent and endurance are maximized by consistent training carried out over a number of years—not months, but years.

Generally, I'm not a faster runner than I was five years ago, but I'm able to run much faster after a long, hard bike ride than I ever thought possible.

As you become more skillful and conditioned in the other two sports, your running will begin to improve again—not as quickly as it might have if you had stuck just with running, nor will it ever get as good as it might have, but you'll become a better runner *as a triathlete*. The muscle groups that control the three sports will develop in an integrated way, to the point where they will eventually balance each other. Your body will begin to accept the idea of having to swim, then bike, then run as a natural process. You'll find, as I did, that your cycling will become easier and better and your running will become easier and better— *together*.

Cyclists or Swimmers with No Running Background

The key to running is to enjoy it. That's a statement that sounds self-contradictory to a nonrunner, I realize. It might even sound a little off to some of you who have been running for years. But running *can* be fun—*should* be fun—if it's approached gently, calmly, and with an open mind. If you've never run more than a mile in your life but are bound and determined to run a 10K in under 35 minutes your first time out, you're doomed.

As an athlete, you are most likely a goal-oriented person. When you begin a running program, goal-setting is important, but you should reverse the direction you're probably used to. Force yourself to run *short distances slowly* at first. Watch the scenery, let your mind wander, smell the flowers. Watch your legs move and listen to your own breathing. Instead of trying to disassociate from an activity you've heard was a drudge, concentrate on enjoying it. That should be your first goal. If you come back from a run exhausted, if the thought of running tomorrow is something you'd rather deal with later, then you've failed.

Start Slowly. Start with a mile, and if that's ridiculously long or short, go a longer or shorter distance. Get to the point where you can run five miles comfortably, without stopping. Then, instead of increasing your distance, begin to run more quickly. Test your limits gradually, but always with a sense of excitement, not dread.

Style. Style is important in running, but make the distinction between your personal style and a style someone has labeled as "ideal." There is no such thing, and most of the material you read on the subject often stretches to make a point. Run the way it feels comfortable to run. Experiment to find the right combination of foot placement and arm movement and stride length, but remember that it's impossible to run in any way that doesn't *feel right*. Trying to do otherwise is not only frustrating; it can also lead to injuries.

Body Types. People get into this thing about body types: "I can't run because I don't have the right body type." Well, that's simply not true. Look at a guy like Rob DeCastella, the Australian who held the world marathon record a few years back. He's got legs like tree trunks, and if he had listened to people hung up on "the perfect running body" when he started, he'd probably have taken up tennis. Runners look like runners mostly because they run a lot. Train hard—train consistently—and you'll look like a triathlete. Be comfortable. Be patient.

Be Careful. If you've been successful in another sport, you will tend to go too hard when you start training to run in triathlons. First, you want to succeed because you're used to succeeding. Second, you're in good cardiovascular shape, so your lungs will adapt easily to the demands of distance running. But it's important to remember that running is much tougher on your body than swimming or cycling. Overdoing it initially can lead to chronic injuries in several areas—ankles, knees, and hips. In this respect, a wealth of natural talent can be a detriment.

The best example of a tremendously talented athlete who went too far too fast is Mark Allen, my former J David teammate and a friend I still often train with. Mark swam in college and was on his way to medical school when he tried his first triathlon—the San Diego USTS race in 1982. He finished fourth behind Dave Scott, Scott Molina, and me. Two months later he won the Horny Toad Triathlon in San Diego, beating both Molina and me. Mark had a great bike ride at that race and was in the lead going into the run, but Scott and I were both sure we could catch him on the run. We didn't. Mark gained ground by running his

Stay off the asphalt and cement. Run the trails whenever possible.

first competitive half-marathon in 75 minutes—in 90-degree heat and after a killer bike ride.

The next year, Mark committed himself full-time to the sport, but he had only those of us who had been competing for a couple of years to use as examples. He trained hard and tried to do the big mileage that everyone else seemed to think was necessary. As a result, he spent almost the entire year recovering from one injury or another. Despite his amazing physical gifts, he really didn't have a good race until the Nice Triathlon in September.

I've never seen anyone who has gone so far as rapidly as Mark, but in 1983 it was almost as if he had gone to graduate school without going to college. Every once in a while he'd get into a course where he needed, say, Biology 101, which he hadn't taken. He didn't have the background; he hadn't built a base, and his body just wasn't yet able to handle the strain.

"I came into the sport with a swimmer mentality," Mark said. "In swimming you go hard on everything, every time you go out there. You just can't do that when you first start out in other sports."

Mark is still known in San Diego as the guy to train with when you want to go hard, but he's much more careful with his racing and training schedule than most of the other top guys in the sport. He has to be. He takes days off from running that Scott Molina and I usually don't, but, if he didn't, he'd be hurt all the time. Mark came into the sport like a flash, and he learned through bad experience the need for patience and moderation, the need to listen to his own body and not to the "experts."

Mark Allen pushed too hard in training and spent most of his first full year recovering from one injury or another.

THE TRAINING PROGRAM

When I started running again after high school in 1976, I ran 65–90 miles a week every week. Usually, it was the same distance day in and day out because I had only so many hours in which to train. I ran for an hour and 15 minutes, give or take, from South Mission Beach in San Diego up the coast to La Jolla and back. If I felt good, I'd run hard; if I felt bad, I'd run slow. Like so many other runners (and if you're an experienced runner, you'll recognize this; if you're not, it's a trap you are almost bound to fall into), I felt that the more miles, the better.

What I didn't know was that I wasn't coming close to maximizing my potential. All those miles were keeping me fit, but no more. Gradually, I learned that fewer miles, run more intelligently, make for a better and more effective program.

Today I'm pretty firm on maintaining a hard day/easy day training schedule. I try to keep my racing and my very intensive workouts separated by at least one day of low-intensity effort. Four different kinds of training make up my week:

The Long Run

Once a week, you should put in a long run at a comfortable pace. This is the basic building block of an endurance program. The run can be as short as 10 miles or as long as 20 or 25. The important thing is that it be at least twice as long as your normal mid-week run.

I do my long runs on Sunday mornings, usually with a group of friends, on a

course with plenty of hills, and I run on dirt trails as much as possible because long runs on hard pavement are an invitation to some sort of stress injury.

Sunday morning runs to me are the best part of the week. Keeping the group noncompetitive is sometimes a problem, but for the most part the pace is easy enough so that everyone is content to talk and explore new trails along the way. Also, the easy pace will encourage runners who may not be going the whole distance to join the group for a portion of the run. The scene shifts, the conversation moves back and forth, and there's a good sense of camaraderie, with no pressure on anyone to go farther than they feel they should.

The long weekly run is important for a couple of reasons. First, as I said, it's a basic part of your endurance program. Your body needs to learn how to run efficiently for long periods of time. And you need to learn what your body requires in order to do that. What and how to eat, what pace to run, what kind of shoes and clothing are best for you, and other questions all have different answers for different bodies. The only way to find out those answers is to put yourself to the test. Reading about how to run 10 or 20 or 30 miles isn't going to help much at all.

Second, the long run is a confidence builder—and confidence is an important part of this business. At first, the simple act of conquering a specific distance will be a thrill, whether you've gone 5 miles or 20. Later, when you've reached a goal distance, getting stronger and faster week after week will assure you that progress is being made.

Rest Runs

Here's where your being comfortable on the run comes in handy. Interspersed between quality workouts, rest runs are nothing more than slow, easy miles that simply keep your legs used to the activity. The goal here is just to maintain the habit; on rest days I go no farther than an easy seven or eight miles. Frank Shorter once told me that it probably would be better not to run at all on rest days, but I'd rather get in the extra miles because I know it will pay off in my ability to recover quickly after a race. The question of whether you should run on a rest day is an individual one, but generally, if going out seems like a chore—if getting out the door is a real effort—it's probably best not to.

Hard Runs

To become stronger and faster, you'll have to include some sort of speed training in your workout schedule. Interval sessions on the track, fartlek runs over any terrain, hill running, and longer, sustained runs over a set distance are four kinds of speed work that I've used successfully over the years. I'll explain each in turn.

As with all other segments of your triathlon training, it's best to work gradually into your speed work—the injury potential is greater when you're running fast. Begin, for example, by planning an interval workout on Tuesdays. Stick with the program and give your body plenty of time to adjust to the

Intervals on the track can make you strong and fast. Many triathletes ignore them and shouldn't.

increased intensity before you add another hard, fast day to your week. Your running will improve as you become a better cyclist and swimmer, and gradually you'll be able to handle tougher workouts in each sport. Gradual progression and consistency are crucial here.

Intervals. Interval training consists of running (or cycling or swimming) a set distance at a set pace and then resting, all within a specific time period. Intervals are used in running to develop leg speed and anaerobic potential, but also to build what I call *strength speed*, a critical capability for triathletes since they're already pretty beaten up by the time they start running.

The difference between building pure speed and building strength speed is the amount of rest you take. If I were looking to get as fast as I could be, I might do 8 × 440 yards with a 440-yard jog in between each. But in a strength workout, I'd do 12 ×440 yards with a 110-yard jog in between—less than a minute rest. I wouldn't be able to run each repeat as fast—perhaps 5–8 percent slower—but I'd be forcing my body to recover faster. I'd be forcing it to run hard even when it was tired.

The ideal interval distance for triathlon training is 440 yards—once around the standard high school or college track. I'll use shorter distances—110s or 220s—in my warm-up, but an endurance athlete doesn't really need the kind of speed they offer. Sometimes I'll throw in a couple of 880s for endurance, but I rarely do 1-mile repeats, because I end up going too slow. There are other kinds of speed work that are better for developing the sustained speed that intervals longer than 440 yards are used to develop.

Fartlek. Fartlek runs are the direct mental opposite of interval workouts on the track. Instead of set distances run within a confined, controlled area, the idea is to take your speed work into the hills and onto the trails. The work comes from Swedish and means, roughly, "speed play." To me, that translates into "sprint when you feel like it." While some runners take their watch along on fartlek runs—going fast for two minutes, say, then going easy for one—I prefer to speed up and hold a hard pace whenever the urge strikes.

Most of my fartlek workouts are done with friends—old teammates from the J David days, whom I've been training with for years: Scott Molina, Gary Peterson, and Mark Allen—on the trails of Rancho Santa Fe, just east of where I live in north San Diego County. We have an informal group that gets together on Tuesday mornings. Typically, we'll warm up for 15–20 minutes, run 45 minutes worth of fartlek, then cool down for 10–15 minutes. It's a long workout, so we're getting endurance training, but there's plenty of speed in there and strength, too, from climbing the hills.

Just as in track intervals, the warm-up before a fartlek run is important; it prevents injuries by getting the blood moving through your legs, and usually after 15 minutes or so you'll feel a lot more like running hard than you did when you started. Toward the end of the workout, throw in a couple of short, hard bursts to see how you're feeling.

When you're all warmed up, work gradually into your first sustained burst. Go hard for about three minutes initially at a pace that will be *really* hard to maintain near the end. This is where running with someone at your own ability

Fast continuous runs best simulate race conditions.

level can help, because he or she will push you without getting too competitive. The thing to avoid is going so hard during the first part of the workout that you can't get to the end. (For me, running with Scott Molina is ideal—he's really smooth, and he doesn't mind running *with* me, whereas Allen doesn't want to be even half a step behind. He *always* wants to be in front.)

Your rest periods in a fartlek workout should take about as much time as you spent going fast. Drop down to a comfortable pace—not a jog, but a pace at which your breathing will gradually lessen in intensity to the point at which you're ready to go hard again by the time, for example, you reach the next big tree or the bottom of the next hill. When we're going hard in Rancho Santa Fe, we might drop from a 5-minute-per-mile pace to a 6:30, which feels like a crawl, although it's still pretty quick—and that's the whole point. Fartlek training—speed work in general—conditions your body *and your mind* to change your preconceptions of what your speed capabilities are.

After the first 15 or 20 minutes of fartlek, reduce the time you go hard, but increase the intensity. Take a little less rest in between fast periods so that you're continually challenging yourself to go a little faster than you think you can and start running hard again before you think you're quite ready.

Toward the end of the workout, run a couple of short blasts. To gauge your progress, time yourself over a part of your fartlek course that you're familiar

Hill running builds strength and speed.

with. A rough mile is a good distance; keep track of your week-to-week progress for comparison's sake.

After the last fast section of your run, take a 10- to 15-minute cool-down, even if you've gone really hard and feel pretty beat. This is an important part of any speed workout because the lactic acid you've produced needs to be cleared out of the muscle tissue by circulated blood. If you sit, or jump right into your car, you'll be stiff and sore the next day, more apt to be injured, and less likely to *want* to go out and train.

You'll find, after you've settled into your routine, that fartlek runs will be one of the highlights of your running program. The best part is that it's the one kind of speed training you can do almost anywhere. It's best in the woods, on the trails, but caught in the middle of a city, you can go hard from stoplight to stoplight or building to building; run fast for four blocks and easy for two.

Hill Running. Running hills is great for building both strength and speed. I'm fortunate that I live in an area in which hills abound—to avoid them takes some doing. If you're in a similar situation, I'd recommend simply incorporating hill running into several of your runs per week. Just go out for five, six miles or more and take the hills as they come.

If the hills where you live are few and far between, then hill repeats are the best thing. You'll need something fairly steep, at least 200 meters long, and if you can find a circuitous route back down that isn't as steep as the way you ran up, then use it. Pounding down the hills in any situation is a great way to come up with a knee or hip injury.

When running hills, stay on your toes as you climb—some good runners actually look like they're bouncing up a hill—and use your arms. Keep your head down but your shoulders high. Concentrate on lifting your knees high. Always run over the top of a hill strongly instead of relaxing (or collapsing). This will add significantly to the training effect.

Hard hill running will take a lot out of the quadriceps muscles in your thighs, so don't do a hill workout if you have a long bike ride planned the next day. Avoid injury by not running hard on the hills two days in a row.

The Fast, Continuous Run. At least twice a month (I make a weekly habit of it), you should simulate race conditions by putting in a fast, sustained run over a set distance. You can do this alone over a course near your home that you're familiar with, but the best way to simulate race conditions I know of is actually to *race.* I wouldn't recommend a triathlon every week unless you've been in the business a while and know you can handle it, but for a triathlete, the weekend 10K is one of the best training tools around. For the price of admission you get a hard 6.2 miles, complete with water, split times, and people to push you. And with a clock at the finish line, the 10K is a perfect time trial—an excellent way to gauge your progress.

"The thing about going really hard is that, no matter what level you're doing it at, if it seems like it's fun—and that's what you're striving for—and if it's something that, in a sense, is *easier* than going easy, then you're going to be OK, and you won't get injured. But I know personally, when I'm trying to go hard and it's drudgery—if having to go hard becomes an obsession—that's when I start to break down and get injured. I've learned to back off when I need to."—Mark Allen

6
BUILDING YOUR PROGRAM

Before you develop a training program, it's necessary to examine your level of motivation: why do you want to become a triathlete in the first place?

If you're new to the sport, this might sound like a funny question. To you, "because it sounds like fun" might be a perfectly good answer. After all, you're not embarking on a new career or enlisting in the military.

On the other hand, an experienced triathlete—at almost any level of participation—probably knows better. This sport does require time and a certain amount of dedication. The happiest triathletes are those who have made training and fitness a part of their lives. The frustrated ones are those whose goals exceed their capabilities in either a physical, an emotional, or a logistical sense.

As in most things, except in a greater and more literal sense, you'll get out of triathloning what you put into it. But it can take away plenty, too. You enjoy challenges, attempting things that those around you might shy away from. Training for and finishing your first race is immensely satisfying, so training for and completing your second is even more so. Suddenly, the idea of missing a workout becomes unthinkable. Pieces of your life that were important before become obstructions—necessary ones, but obstructions nonetheless—and you've become Mr. Type A in a matter of months, filled with guilt about the things you should do, the miles you should be putting in. You're in great shape, but you're not really healthy.

First, then, decide why you want to become a triathlete. Do you simply want to lose weight, or would you like to win the Ironman? Does training look like fun, or is training just a way to expand your commitment to fitness? Many

Why be a triathlete? Staying superfit is one good reason.

triathletes originally got into the sport for the challenge, then stayed in because of the physical and psychological rewards, so it's very likely your original motivation will change. Define one, anyway. It will help you keep things in focus.

The next point is to set a goal for yourself. Keep it simple and relatively short-range. Perhaps you've just seen your first triathlon, and there's another one in town in six months. Perfect. Or maybe you'd like to place well in your age group in the next race.

Personally, I've always had better success by keeping long-term goals somewhat vague because I know they're going to change. I keep a general, long-range plan in my head, but it's never something that will make me feel uncomfortable if I don't achieve it. Instead, I focus on the next race or, at most, a couple of major races during the season. Then I have plenty of room to adjust along the way.

The best analogy I can make here is the way many good marathoners run their races. Focusing on the finish line when it's still miles away only makes the race seem longer. Instead, they set little minor goals for themselves along the way: they run from one corner to the next or from the bottom of the next hill to the top. Each goal they achieve makes them more confident about being able to achieve another, and they are able to maintain a high level of intensity over a period of time that might have looked impossible when they started.

Once you've answered the question "Why?" and you've set an initial goal, you'll have to conduct a physical self-test to evaluate your current level of conditioning. If you're already training and competing in triathlons, you'll be able to be more specific in your analysis: Can you handle the weekly 20-mile run you'll need before you can move to longer-distance triathlons? Is getting faster in short triathlons a priority, but do your legs get wobbly after one or two hard 440s on the track?

If you're already a good runner, the triathlon self-test might be an eye-opener. Try swimming. Surely a mile in the pool can't be all that bad. So you join the local Masters swim program, and within a thousand yards you're gasping for air and hanging on to the side of the pool for dear life. "But I run a 2:28 marathon!" you protest. "I'm in great shape!" The question is "For what?" There's more to this business than meets the eye.

If you've decided to start training, and you've done little or nothing that is strenuous for years and are over 40 and overweight, don't take a step until you've had your doctor give you the OK. Challenges are heroic, and there's a lot of mind over matter in triathlons, but it only goes so far. The tragedy of the late Jim Fixx taught us that "fitness" is a relative term at best. If you have any doubt about your ability to handle the training, if running or cycling results in chest pains or dizziness or prolonged fatigue, spend a few bucks and have a stress test and an EKG done. If nothing else, it will put your mind at ease.

Getting Down to Business

There's no way you can tell in advance how good a triathlete you can be by listening to an expert or reading a chart. How many potential world-class cyclists are floating around who have never ridden a bike? How many Olympic gold medal swimmers have been born who have never learned to swim? Triathlon is a new sport in which frontiers are continuously being explored. The only way for *you* to explore yourself as a triathlete is to jump in and go.

After you've set a goal, sketched out your motivation, and gauged your physical condition, take a good look at your average day and decide how many hours you're willing to devote to training. I could suggest a minimum of two, four, or six hours a day, but how could a single suggestion suffice for a 22-year-old lifeguard, an ex-collegiate swimmer, and a 45-year-old executive who hasn't been on a bike in 15 years?

Generally, I would say that a bare minimum of one-and-a-half to two hours of training a day is necessary for you to be able to complete what are commonly referred to as "short-distance" triathlons. Good examples of races at this distance are the events of the Bud Light U.S. Triathlon Series, which features a swim of 1.5 kilometers (.9 miles), a 40-kilometer bike ride (24.8 miles), and a 10-kilometer run (6.2 miles). You won't be able to *race* them with that amount of training, but you'll be comfortable getting from the start to the finish; the sport will be fun, and that's a great place to start.

Commitment Is the Key

Regardless of where you begin—with humble thoughts of merely finishing a triathlon or realistic plans for becoming a world champion—following through on your first estimate of available training time is critical. No factor has been more important for me than simply staying with my program month after month, year after year. That's why I suggest in the first place that you look hard at your level of interest. You won't be eager to train every day, but the overall routine must be rewarding. If it becomes a grind, then you'll never stick with the sport long enough to see real results.

SCHEDULING YOUR WORKOUTS

Swimming

The first thing you should do, regardless of your background, is to find a local Masters swim program and join it. Of all three sports, swimming is the one that depends most on coaching and supervised workouts. Also, because of competitive swimming's reliance on interval training, there's almost no way for you to train as hard as you need to without having someone stand on the deck, running the old pace clock and urging you on. Lap after lap of solo distance work in the pool or a summer's worth of swimming from buoy to buoy in the ocean or the nearest lake simply will not develop your ability past a very basic point. Remember, the goal is not simply to survive a mile in the open water; you have to come out in good enough shape to jump on your bike and go.

Plan to swim at least three times a week, a minimum of 1,500 yards per workout. Don't think about doing anything but intervals; 100s, 200s (yards) at first, then a combination of everything from fast 50s to 800s as you build up. In my opinion, Mondays, Wednesdays, and Fridays are the best days, because you can head right to work after practice. Or head to practice right after work. Evenings are perhaps the best because, first of all, the pool *feels* good after work. Second, darkness often gets to be a problem for either running or biking, but swimming at night, even outdoors, is no problem.

Reserve at least an hour for each session, or perhaps a little extra, so there will be plenty of time for a warm-up, a cool-down, and the drive to the pool and back again. Taking into account time for traveling is important. It's kind of like adding the interest to the cost of buying a new car—it's not on the sticker, but it's a big part of the deal.

For the experienced swimmer or athlete who is trying to build a competitive program, five days in the pool are essential, with a race or a long swim in the ocean or a lake on weekends, weather permitting. Build to where you can handle 15,000–25,000 yards a week, then concentrate on getting faster by swimming your base distance harder and leaving less time for rest in between.

Whatever your level of skill, you'll find that you won't need to allot more time for your workout as you get better; you'll simply squeeze more and better-quality mileage into your allotted time in the pool.

Biking

No one in his or her right mind cycles in the dark—at least not at night (predawn bicycle rides are almost a way of life for some triathletes pressed for training time)—so write a minimum of three days per week on your bike into your schedule after you arrange for the swimming. Leave your running routine for last.

Remember that biking will be the most time-consuming portion of your training. On nonswimming days you'll be able to put in an hour or so before work, but the bulk of your cycling mileage will most likely be covered on weekends. Plan to ride on Wednesdays, do your long ride (three to four hours at first) on Saturdays, and do a medium ride on Sundays. Your total bike mileage will depend on how many miles you run each week; for a balanced program, you should ride six times as many miles as you run.

Of the three sports, cycling is probably going to be the toughest to fit into your schedule. In swimming, there's the peer pressure of the group you're training with to keep you going. And you can *run* anywhere at any time. With cycling, though, there's more gear to put on; there are tires to pump and chains to spray, and more attention must be paid to the environment. Creativity is the only way out.

Commuting to work by bike is an excellent way to get in the mileage without straining your schedule. If you're within an hour's drive from where you work (and most of us are), then commuting is a possibility. Keep in mind the drive/bike ratio I mentioned in Chapter 4: two hours of cycling for every hour in the car in normal city traffic.

The best time for your Saturday long ride is early in the morning. Most of the rest of the world is still asleep, the stores aren't open, and you'll find that the 40 or 50 miles will go quickly without traffic coming at you from all sides. An early start will also save the rest of the day for other things. With all your swimming workouts for the week behind you and a long run scheduled for Sunday, the pressure is off. Begin at 6:00 A.M., get off the bike at 10:00, and you've still got all the time you need to mow the lawn, take the kids to the zoo, whatever. Once again, if you're going to enjoy this sport, and the people around you are going to

Your weekly long run
is the foundation of an
endurance running program.

enjoy it with you, then your training must *fit* into your life. If you try to jam it into cracks where it doesn't belong, everyone will lose.

The 6:1 bike/run ratio I mentioned above generally holds true for top triathletes, too, although biking is usually a seven-day-a-week proposition. In full-time triathlon training, expect to put in 300–450 miles a week, with a long ride of over 100 miles on Saturday or Sunday.

Running

Since most triathletes come from a running background, the biggest problem in this category is holding people back. If you've got plenty of experience under your belt—if 50 miles a week, say, is fairly standard for you—lower it to 30 and concentrate on balancing your program in all three sports before moving up in distance. One of the nicest things about cross-training in several disciplines is a reduction in the number of running-related injuries most people suffer, but if you hold to your running peak and try to throw two more activities into an already full barrel, *something* is going to give.

If you have little or no background in running, set your swimming and biking at reasonable levels, then hold them there while your running catches up. Minimum mileage? Four days a week for a total of at least 20 miles. Bear in mind that even the strongest and the best in this sport rarely run over 80.

In a basic triathlon training program, run on Tuesdays, Thursdays, Fridays, and Sundays. If you've been keeping track of what you've read so far (if not, refer to the chart at the end of this chapter), you'll note that on Tuesdays and Thursdays running is *all* you do, so concentrate on quality. The runs on these days should tax you, either because you've run a basic distance quickly or because you've put in a track or a fartlek workout.

Friday should be an easy run day, a rest day on which you run just to get some miles in. You've run that morning and run hard the day before; you're going to be going long on the bike tomorrow and long on the run on Sunday.

Your long run on Sunday should be at least twice as long as the race you are planning on entering or twice as long as your average daily run. Test your limits gently; if your longest weekly run is 6 miles, go 13 on Sunday, keeping in mind that your only workout on Monday will be in the pool.

PITFALLS TO WATCH FOR

Overtraining

Overtraining is the hidden enemy of all endurance athletes, whether they are middle-of-the-packers or contenders at the front. The very reason people get involved in this sport is that they seek to achieve. What better way to achieve than to do more, harder, longer than anyone else?

In 1985, I spent almost the entire second half of the season overtrained. I had my best races early. Looking back, I probably peaked in June at the Ironman-distance Midwest Classic in Minnesota, which I won over Scott Molina. After that, it was all downhill.

Scott and I both raced hard in that event, but I felt good the next day, so I went out and swam and cycled. Two days later I did an 80-mile bike ride. All this after nine hours of racing. Big mistake.

The next weekend was the Bud Light USTS race in Portland, which I passed up, but which Scott won. That worried me. If he's recovered enough to do that, I thought, then *I* must be recovered, too. But everyone is different. What I should have done was back off completely for a couple of days and come back gradually. Instead, I pushed when I should have pulled. From that point in the season on, I made gradual progress—in the wrong direction.

As you build your program, be aware that overtraining can occur at all levels. Neither the established star nor the beginner is immune. Have the courage to be able to act on what your body is telling you it needs; take a break when taking a break sounds like the best thing in the world and a five-mile run sounds like the worst. All of the following are signs that you may need to sit the next one out:

- lack of motivation
- loss of weight despite the fact that you're eating like a horse
- loss of appetite despite consistent training
- a significant rise in your normal pulse rate upon waking
- sleeplessness despite the fact that you're tired
- general feeling of sluggishness
- slow recovery from workouts or races

Stagnation

Your progress as you begin to train for triathlons will be rapid, at least in the sports you are new to. Your times in swimming will drop rapidly, hills that you thought were mountains a month before on the bike don't even slow you down. The first few months of training will fill you full of high expectations.

The other side of the coin is that, once you reach certain levels, stagnation will occur. Your times for 100-yard intervals will hang in one spot for weeks, perhaps longer. Your time trials on the bike will sit as if they were inscribed on the face of the watch.

Performance plateaus are a natural part of any athlete's life, which doesn't make them any easier to deal with. In some cases, simple patience is the answer. In others, creativity in structuring your program can break the logjam wide open.

If you've hit a wall with your running, for example, substitute a track workout for your fartlek run. Or run in the mornings instead of at lunch. On the bike, take one day a week and spend 30 minutes on an indoor trainer. For me, swimming with hand paddles for a month resulted in a big drop in my times. Bodies are funny—you never know what they are going to respond to. The thing you don't want to do is give up. Never resign yourself to the "fact" that you won't get any faster, because the next, higher plateau might be just around the corner. Once again, those two key words crop up: patience, consistency.

OFF TO THE RACES

Your First Triathlon

We've talked about setting short-range goals, which usually revolve around a race in the not-too-distant future. How do you know you're ready?

Well, you may be ready now. If you're in reasonably good shape, even if you haven't put in any training specific to the triathlon, there are short races out there waiting. Mini-triathlons with swims of 400 yards or less, bike rides of 10 miles or less, runs of only a couple of miles, will not only give you a thrilling introduction into the sport, but they'll offer a beginner a heck of a sense of accomplishment. More than one avid triathlete began his or her racing career by plunging into a very short event with little or no training.

When the distances get longer—a mile swim, a 25-mile bike, and a 10K run, like the Bud Light U.S. Triathlon Series events—a little more planning and

**Your first race:
keep it short, keep it fun.**

preparation are needed. It's difficult to make a generalization here, so the best way to determine if you are ready is to check the training of people you know who have completed similar races. Chances are, if you've been putting in a couple of hours a day for three months, you've got plenty of margin for error.

The signs that you are *not* ready to compete are any acute fears over any one of the three legs of a triathlon. If you've been training in a pool for six months, but have yet to swim in the open water without getting panicky, then there's more work to do. If you're very shaky on your bike in crowds, then perhaps you'd better get in a few group training rides before you sign up to compete.

Keep in mind that the mental game in triathlons is important. If you *think* you can, you probably will. If you doubt too much, reinforce the weak spots before you toe the line.

Long- and Ultra-Distance Programs

Here's where the idea of fitting your training into your life begins to fall apart. For events of half-Ironman (long) or Ironman (ultra) duration—races that will take you anywhere from 5 or 6 hours to 10, 12, or more hours to finish—a major training commitment is necessary. While you can struggle through a half-Ironman-distance triathlon on less than two hours of training a day, it's likely that your feeling of accomplishment for having done so will be tempered by your being miserable for most of the race. There is some truth in the "gruel-a-thon" image of the triathlon, but a large part of it is due to marginally prepared athletes competing over their heads at distances beyond their capabilities.

Generally, in preparing for a long-distance triathlon, you should think in terms of doubling the base mileages that we talked about earlier in this chapter. That means three to four hours of training per day, with double workouts—swim/bike, run/bike, etc.—almost daily. Your over-distance runs must reach into the 15-mile range, and your long bike rides will climb toward 80.

The sport is full of athletes who began their involvement by successfully completing ultra-distance triathlons. It's advisable, though, to give yourself some room. Unless you come recently from a strong competitive background in one of the three sports with high aspirations of becoming a triathlon champion, you should spend your first year building your program and competing in short-distance events. Training counts for a lot in triathloning, but experience does, too. The more comfortable you are with the logistics of competing in three sports, the greater your chance of success when you do enter an ultra-.

With your goal set on the Ironman Triathlon in Hawaii or a race of similar distance, most of the rest of your life goes on hold. You've got a year or more of competition at lesser distances under your belt, and you understand the mechanics of day-in, day-out training. Either you're in the luxurious position of having flexible work hours or you've already experimented with pigeonholing training into odd hours of the day, like biking to and from work, running during lunch, biking back and forth from the pool, and so on.

For the moderately trained triathlete, I would recommend starting your ultra-distance program at least six months from race day. The prospect of 11, 12, or

15 hours of constant competition should not be taken lightly. Most of the people who have come away from their first Hawaii Ironman, for instance, with good feelings are those who went in simply *appalled* at the challenge, and who *trained* as if they were.

Work at a program that is based on consistency and lots of good mileage—especially on the bike, because the bike ride in Hawaii is just *awesome*. Gradually increase the intensity and length of your workouts with an eye toward injury prevention and become familiar with techniques and equipment that will make your job easier. The Ironman-in-training who wastes time and energy finding his or her one pair of cycling shorts in the morning, or who breaks a worn shoelace in the rush of getting out the door before work, is putting needless strain on his or her program.

Personally, I think the peripheral frustrations are what burn out people in heavy training, *not* the mileage. Stress can lead you into overtraining just as easily as too many long runs. Streamline your ultra-distance routine with good equipment and forethought.

The finish at the 1982 Ironman.

ALTERNATIVE FORMS OF TRAINING

How do you deal with day-in, day-out training without frying your brain to a crisp with boredom? Varying the intensity of your workouts certainly is one method. An easy day makes you ready for a hard day, which makes you anxious for an easy day. One day you run hills, the next day you ride the flats, and so on.

Still, it can get tedious. When it does, lighthearted training alternatives can get you back on track. Once in a while it's nice to stop and remember what got you hooked in the first place: that working out is fun.

Competition in sports in which you have no particular vested interest can be a real joy. If you belong to a Masters swim program, enter a couple of events in the next meet. Swim the distance freestyle races for training, then jump into the breaststroke or the backstroke just for fun. Whether you perform well or not is hardly the issue—you may find the freedom from the *pressure* to do so to be refreshing.

Actually, competition in any form of organized swimming is great for a triathlete because, of all the three sports, this is the one that inspires the most anxiety. Competitive open-water swims are an excellent way to improve your skills and build your confidence. Don't race unless you're comfortable and fast enough to do so. Instead, just participate. Concentrate on staying smooth and watch how the experts work.

In the absence of organized competition, group swims can help you become comfortable in the open water. One Masters swimming team in San Diego meets during the summer at a beautiful public beach in La Jolla at around 6:00 P.M. Team members, families, and friends arrive gradually over the course of an hour and then break up informally into smaller groups by ability level. Everyone swims a mile or so, then dries off and enjoys what has become a regular Friday night dinner at the park, complete with blankets, barbecue grill, and beer.

You can compete in organized cycling, too, although you should be warned in advance: in my experience there's almost never *anything* casual about organized cycling. Stay away from road races—you'll need a license, a category assignment, and a suit of armor. Enter public-entry time trials, where it's just you against the clock. The competitive atmosphere will get you going harder than you might in a solo workout, and the time at the finish line will give you a good gauge to measure yourself against next time out.

Training vacations can break up the routine effectively, too. Take off on your bicycle into the mountains for a couple of days with a few friends. Camp out or stay in a motel and use your training—your running or your cycling—to explore new surroundings. I've been on plenty of runs in park areas where I went much farther and faster than I had intended to go simply because I was enjoying the environment and the company.

Offbeat workouts, with little structure, are really the best wherever you are. They can combine a change in scenery with a new physical challenge, and, best of all, thoughts of time and distance are far removed. If the realization that you've just taxed the heck out of your body doesn't occur until after you've stopped laughing, then the workout has been a success.

The point is that this is hardly a sport that you can take seriously *all* the time. Use your imagination and remember that even the best need a break from pumping up and down the same stupid hills day after day after day.

The following piece, part of which was published in *City Sports Monthly* in 1985, is about an unconventional event called a "Ride & Tie," that has become somewhat of a fixture in the San Diego area over the last couple of years. Put on by a guy named Bob Babbitt on a very irregular basis (we do count on him for an Easter Ride & Tie and a Thanksgiving Ride & Tie), the events have remained doggedly casual in all respects. There is definitely no schedule. Babbitt makes a couple of phone calls, and the word spreads. The regular faces are always ready for more, and newcomers are always welcome.

When we left Bob Babbitt and Scott Tinley, they were running painfully along the Queen Kahahumanu Highway, just outside of the little town of Kailua-Kona on the Big Island of Hawaii. The temperature was 90 degrees, the humidity was close to that, and both men, given the opportunity, could probably have found a better way to spend a Saturday afternoon than competing in the 1984 Ironman.

Babbitt, a bearded 32-year-old former grade-school physical education instructor, was woefully unprepared for the event. Undertrained and slightly undermotivated, barely able to walk through a marathon, let alone run it, he was three hours behind the pace he'd set for himself at the Ironman in '82.

Tinley, the Ironman champ February 1982 and the only man ever to beat Dave Scott in this event, was farther along in the field and feeling much better, but it had been a bad day. He'd been talked out of quitting completely during the bike and by now was willing to settle for what everyone all day had been trying to give him: second place.

It is now seven months later. The scene is San Diego, and the temperature is more bearable. In fact, it's balmy—ideal for almost anything except ice skating and conquering towering Himalayan peaks. Daylight savings time has just recently gone into effect, so at 5:30 in the evening on Friday, May 4, 1984, the sun is still high, casting a golden glow on the surrounding hills, which are covered with scrub grasses, bright yellow mustard, and stunted live oak.

Babbitt and Tinley are not alone. Around them is an odd mixture of 20 or so athletes, several of them women, half of them astride bicycles that bear little resemblance to the sleek 12-speeds one normally associates with the triathlon community in southern California. The bikes are, in fact, humble beach cruisers, lacking only the Styrofoam beer cup on the handlebars for full, weekend-ready authenticity.

For several years now, Babbitt has been organizing informal races called Ride & Ties, after the better-known horse-and-rider affairs sponsored by the Levi-Strauss Company.

Babbitt's events utilize two leapfrogging teammates and a bike rather than a horse, but the technique is the same. Everyone starts out at the same time, with the cyclist pumping on up ahead. Leaving the bike alongside of the road at an obvious or prearranged spot, the first cyclist then runs on. His or her partner, still on foot, finds the bike, mounts up, and pedals into the lead, leaving the bike at the next drop, and so on.

In the original version, the horse was tied to a tree or bush; hence the name. At Babbitt's races the bikes were originally locked, but that took too much time—the machines are now simply left by the side of the road along with the implied hope that they don't get stolen. In several years, that's never happened, although the vulnerability has left the bikes open to pranksters like Tinley, who have been known to ride off with another team's bike, relocate it behind a bush or remove a wheel, and hide *that*. Still, it's better than horses, safer on one hand—no one gets bitten or thrown—and cheaper—bikes need only a cleaning and some grease every week or so and not so much as a stalk of hay in between.

This particular Ride & Tie is different, however. It is Babbitt's inaugural cross-country event, with borrowed cruisers instead of racing bikes and lots of hills and trails and dust instead of asphalt and cement.

"The turnaround is out there somewhere," Babbitt tells the field, many of whom are rolling back and forth on their bikes at the starting line, apprehensively testing coaster breaks for the first time since they were 10-year-olds. "Just follow the trail. There are a couple of forks, but you shouldn't miss the main one. If you do . . . well, I guess you'll be lost."

Babbitt doesn't stand on formality at any of his Ride & Ties, and at this one he's even more relaxed than usual.

"How far *is* the turnaround?" comes a question.

"Uh, five, six miles," replies Babbitt. "Somewhere around that. Everybody ready?"

Everyone is, so off they bounce, half on foot, half on the bikes.

The first part of Babbitt's course is flat, leading into an undeveloped area north of San Diego proper called Sorrento Valley. There are no cars, no intersections, no traffic lights. There are cows, though, and cow pies on the trail that the competitors dodge or don't, depending on their (the pies, of course) stage of dehydration. The cows just stand their ground in the fields on either side of the trail and watch, moolessly.

Two miles out, the hills begin, and the athletes discover the difficulty of going up, steeply, without being able to switch gears. The tough guys stand on their pedals and grunt; the smart ones jump off and push. By the third hill, everyone has adopted the second technique.

Going down is harder. The best way is to let the bike roll and skid and bounce at will, with only a gentle touch on the brakes to control the descent. To do that, though, experience on a beach cruiser or an off-road bike is necessary. Few competitors have much of that, so what most do is brake like crazy all the way down the short, steep, rocky grades—a technique that causes the rear wheel of the bike to try to become the *front* wheel, which in turn leads to a fall or at least a good scare.

Better the uphills.

For close to two hours the athletes sweat and strain over the course, bouncing along on fat tires four times as wide as the ones they are used to seeing in front of them. The race for the top spot and first prize—Babbitt's highly coveted, homemade aluminum foil Ride & Tie belt—is tight.

Finally, Colin Brown, a local triathlete with a national reputation, and his brother Barry, clinch first place when Tinley, laughing, falls off his bike at the bottom of the last steep hill, then stops a mile farther on to chase the cows.

"God, I'm sore," says Tinley's partner Jim Reilly as he finishes. "This is worse than the *army!*"

"Fun," says Tinley. "This is much better than the ones we do on the road."

"Better than Ironman, too," says Bob Babbitt. "Let's eat!"

TRAINING MILEAGE GUIDE

The chart on the next page offers some specific mileage guidelines for 10 goal/ ability levels. Levels 7–10 encompass sufficient mileage for ultra-distance training, but can certainly be considered a week-in, week-out program for the serious athlete, with some adjustments six to eight weeks out from a race of any one specific distance—more speed, for instance, prior to a short race; a couple of longer runs and rides prior to an ultra.

Once again I'll strike the theme: *consistency*. If you can make one of these levels work for you on a regular basis, then you've become a triathlete who stands a good chance of staying a triathlete for a long time to come. It's the long-term training effects that will make you strong. Not even the most talented can come right out of the blocks and race well time after time without years of work behind them.

Here's a breakdown of ability levels:

1. The triathlon beginner with little or no experience or the confirmed survivor whose only need is to participate. Responsibilities and commitments other than triathlon have priority.

2. Some athletic background. Has completed his or her first triathlon and is giving serious thought to subscribing to *Triathlon Magazine*.

3. Has the time and the will to train seriously. Spouse is beginning to get the point and begins to give triathlon equipment as presents for birthdays and Christmas. Subscribes to *Triathlon Magazine* and to *Tri-Athlete*.

4. Has several races, perhaps several years of experience, behind him or her. Feels comfortable about walking into a bike store and saying, "gear ratio." Bedtime is 9:30.

5. Has serious thoughts about winning an age group award at the next race. This is a good, solid level for the experienced triathlete with a firm commitment. He or she probably swims with a Masters team in the morning and has gone to great lengths to fit the mileage into the workday.

6. The sport has become *the* number one priority. Family and friends either understand or don't, but the training goes on. The athlete at this level often shows up at work, and leaves work, in training gear.

7. Has lots of experience and is probably training for the Ironman. This person has probably finished near the top in his or her age group. Probably has two bikes and several dresser drawers full of beat-up bike shorts, tights, and T-shirts.

8. Almost a full-time athlete now, taken over by training. Either is retired and very wealthy or works part-time to support his or her training and is very poor. His or her social life has shrunk to almost nothing with good reason—the phone is disconnected after 8:30 P.M.

9. Spouse left long ago. There's no turning back. Is there a sponsor out there somewhere who can help? Is competing in prize money races and has a good chance of taking some of it home.

10. Over the edge. Rent and assorted bills are paid with prize money checks and sponsor support, or they aren't paid at all. Long ago stopped feeling guilty

about his or her daily lap. Fears a debilitating injury more than death by fire. Is a little burned out at times and ponders a quiet life in the mountains, but, what the hell—*someone* has to be a professional triathlete!

Key: (D)—distance   (H)—hard, steady
        (I) —intervals   (R)—recovery

LEVEL		M	TU	W	TH	F	SA	SU	TOTAL	
1	SWIM	1200(H)	0	1800(I)	0	1500(I)	0	0	4500	YD
	BIKE	0	15(H)	0	15(I)	0	25(D)	15(R)	70	MI
	RUN	4(R)	0	6(I)	6(I)	4(H)	0	8(D)	22	MI
2	SWIM	1300(H)	0	2000(I)	0	1600(I)	0	0	4900	YD
	BIKE	0	20(H)	0	20(I)	0	35(D)	20(R)	95	MI
	RUN	5(R)	0	7(I)	0	5(H)	0	9(D)	25	MI
3	SWIM	1500(I)	0	2000(I)	0	1600(I)	750(R)	0	5850	YD
	BIKE	0	25(H)	0	25(I)	0	45(D)	25(R)	120	MI
	RUN	5(R)	0	8(I)	6(H)	0	11(D)	0	30	MI
4	SWIM	1750(I)	0	2200(I)	0	1750(I)	1000(R)	0	6700	YD
	BIKE	0	30(D)	0	35(H)	0	50(D)	25(R)	140	MI
	RUN	5(R)	0	8(I)	0(I)	7(H)	0	13(D)	33	MI
5	SWIM	2000(I)	0	2500(I)	0	2000(I)	1000(R)	0	7500	YD
	BIKE	0	35(D)	0	35(H)	0	55(D)	30(R)	155	MI
	RUN	6(R)	0	9(I)	0	8(H)	0	15(D)	38	MI
6	SWIM	2250(I)	1500(R)	0	2800(I)	2250(I)	1000(R)	0	9700	YD
	BIKE	20(R)	40(D)	0	40(H)	0	60(D)	30(R)	190	MI
	RUN	6(R)	0	9(I)	0	8(H)	0	16(D)	39	MI
7	SWIM	2500(I)	1750	0	3000(I)	2500(I)	1000(R)	0	10,750	YD
	BIKE	25(R)	0	45(D)	50(H)	0	75(D)	30(R)	225	MI
	RUN	7(R)	9(I)	0	7(R)	9(H)	0	16(D)	48	MI
8	SWIM	3000(I)	2000(R)	0	3500(I)	3000(I)	0	1500(R)	13,000	YD
	BIKE	40(D)	20(R)	55(D)	60(H/I)	0	80	35(R)	290	MI
	RUN	0	10(I)	4(R)	9(H)	6(R)	10(H)	18(D)	87	MI
9	SWIM	3500(I)	3000(I)	2000(R)	400(I)	3500(I)	0	1500(R)	17,500	YD
	BIKE	60(D)	35(R)	75(D)	40(R)	50(H/I)	90(D)	0	350	MI
	RUN	0	12(I)	6(R)	10(H)	6(R)	10(H)	20(D)	64	MI
10	SWIM	4500(I)	4500(I)	2000(R)	4500(I)	4500(I)	0	2000(R)	22,500	YD
	BIKE	70(D)	40(R)	85(D)	45(R)	60(H/I)	100(D)	0	400	MI
	RUN	4(R)	13(I)	6(R)	11(H)	6(R)	10(H)	20(D)	70	MI

Keeping A Training Log. Runners keep great training logs. I think it must be their personalities. Norm Green, a bespectacled, goateed, but nonetheless youthful-looking Baptist clergyman from Wayne, Pennsylvania, who holds about every world record there is to hold in road racing for men 50 years and older, keeps a log that would put the financial books of a major accounting firm to shame. Every single workout he's done since he started running seriously in 1968 is in his little black book (or the appropriate volume of his little black book library, at least), recorded in a painstakingly fine hand in black ink, with the pace per mile of each workout in red.

Green's log is neater, better organized, and more comprehensive than most, but it's not unusual within the running community.

Triathletes, on the other hand, are constantly on the *verge* of starting a training log that will put everyone else in the field to shame. In the meantime, records are kept here and there throughout the house, on odd scraps of paper or in several different notebooks that never end up within 20 yards of each other at the same time.

Logs can be a big help when kept consistently. Over a period of time, patterns will develop that can help you know what to eat and when, how to taper, and even what time of the month or year you seem to train and race most efficiently. Every detail of daily life, directly related to your training or not, is fair game for the log—even the most insignificant routine, regularly recorded, can offer fascinating insights when viewed in retrospect.

On the other hand, logs can be dangerous. In the hands of the wrong person they can assume a life of their own, demanding constant attention and a regular flow of data, then spewing back nothing but guilt. I've known runners who will go out on a run Sunday night just so the weekly numbers will add up to expectations. The unforgiving glare of a disappointed log is simply too great a burden for them to face.

I used to keep a log, but I found that after running, biking, and swimming all day, the thought of sitting down each night and writing about it was just another obligation. Plus, I felt that keeping a formal log stripped some of the spontaneity away from my training.

For the inexperienced triathlete—the beginner or the person intent on rapid improvement—I think keeping a log is important. Your memory is never as good as you think it is. Then, again, the day is never as long as you would like it to be, so start your log with time economy in mind. Isolate the details you think are important, then be consistent in recording them. Don't get slavish or compulsive—if the book starts telling you what *it* wants you to do, you're ready for a day or two on the sidelines.

"I felt fine coming off the bike, so I went out at a 7:30 pace. Maybe if I had felt a little crummier, I would have taken it easier. But I felt great, so I went out great.

"At about the six-mile mark, there was Pat Hines on a slight upgrade, barely moving. My first thought was, 'My God, that's too bad.' But I told myself just to blaze by her and keep going. When I passed her, I pushed up the hill to show her: 'Listen, I'm gone. Don't think you can catch me.'

'I'd never been number one before. In all the triathlons I'd done, I'd come in third, second. . . . First was nothing I'd experienced before. Maybe if I had, who knows? It really kept me pushing hard."—Julie Moss speaking of her historic 1982 Ironman.

7
RACING STRATEGY

Don't be put off by the title of this chapter; race strategy is for everyone, whether you're a professional racing for money or a middle-of-the-pack triathlete competing for fun.

Thinking about what you're doing in a competitive environment can make the difference between *having* fun and merely going along for the ride. And say what you will about not caring about your performance—you wouldn't be reading this book if there wasn't something inside of you that wants to make the most out of the tools you've been given. Knowing what you're doing on racing day and having at least an idea of what you *plan* to do adds significantly to the triathlon experience.

But why race at all? For some, that's a good question. I know people who simply enjoy the training and have no psychological need to sign the bottom line of an entry form once every couple of weeks. For most of us, though, formal competition provides benefits in several areas, with the most important factor being its provision of a goal for all of our efforts. "Racing is like taking a formal exam in school," says Tom Warren. "You put a lot of time in studying—the only way to find out where you really stand is to take the test."

THE DAY BEFORE THE RACE

Organization and preparation are the first ingredients of racing strategy. A lot of triathletes who see themselves as experienced take standard necessities like

Heading off to the next event— keep your head up and know the course.

registration, picking up numbers, and checking out technical details of the course or race day schedules lightly. I don't. I actually keep a list of things I need to do the day before the race: do I need to check in the day before? Where do the numbers need to be placed? If I'm staying in a hotel, how will I get to the race site? Are there last-minute changes in the course?

Know the Course

One of the most important things you can do on the day before the race is to go over the course. I *always* do. It's a nightmare not knowing where you're going during a race. Getting lost, especially on the bike, is a very real possibility in many races, even if you're not up in front.

At the Mighty Hamptons Triathlon on Long Island, New York, in 1982, I was a minute and a half behind Dave Scott and moving up when I came to a corner where a little Boy Scout was standing. He yelled something that I didn't hear as I went by, and it was only when a friend told me that I'd missed the turn—a half-mile and three minutes later—that I realized what the little boy had said: "Are you in the race?" My number must have been tucked inside my shirt or something. Whatever, the moral of the story is to know where you're going. And *ride* both the run and the cycling courses if you can; driving over the route in a car can be deceptive.

(Then again, knowing the course *too* well has backfired at least once. At the Nice Triathlon in France in 1983, the Americans trained for a week on the course that had been outlined by race officials. There were two loops at the top of a long straightaway leading out of town: one long loop leading through the mountains up to the little town of Aspremont and a shorter loop that climbed to St. Jeanette. The shorter loop was supposed to be ridden first during the race, but the *gendarmes* mistakenly sent cyclists toward the big loop first. Everyone obeyed except John Howard and another American, George Yates, who, *knowing* the right way, insisted on following it. They both lost lots of time in the confusion. Worse, volunteers at the aid stations refused to believe they were in the race. Race officials refused to consider their protests after the event.)

Don't ignore the swim course prior to the event. While it's rare that a race director will place buoys the day before the event, check out the general area. Ask lifeguards about water conditions: general temperature, warm spots or cold spots, surf, and currents. I watched a triathlete in a local San Diego event one year let the entire pack go into the water, then sprint 50 yards down the beach, jump in, and ride a rip current he'd seen earlier all the way to a 30-yard lead at the first buoy.

Check the swim course thoroughly and carefully. Know where the buoys are.

Train with your equipment. Plan ahead, so that you won't fumble around during a race.

Equipment

There's not much you can do 30 minutes before the race if you find that you've brought only one cycling shoe. Go over your equipment the day before the race. This sounds like a matter of simple common sense, and it is, but it's also a point forgotten by even the most experienced triathletes. A checklist is best—keep one handy and use it. We'll go over specific equipment in Chapter 9.

Tapering

This is a most inexact science, but an important one. All the care and preparation in the world, combined with the wisest race-day strategy, won't be worth a thing if your legs don't work after a week of heavy, prerace training.

There are no hard and fast rules about how to taper for a triathlon. Common sense will tell you that a hard 100-mile bike ride on the Saturday before a Sunday race won't do you much good. On the other hand, if you race frequently, your total training program can take a nosedive because you're constantly tapering.

If you plan on racing frequently, set up your schedule early in the season and determine which races are particularly important. Ease off three or four days before those and lighten up for only a day before the others. Most importantly, stick to your schedule (allow for minor adjustments, of course), because short-term tapering benefits are hard to evaluate. So many cirucumstances enter into what makes you feel good or bad on race day that a consistent period of self-analysis is critical. Even then, it's easy to get thrown off track; tapering is a delicate combination of experience, intuition, guilt, and 11th-hour nerves. Perhaps the best way of all to go into a big race is to have a week of light training directly behind you, a ton of hard stuff behind that, and a panicky feeling, the night before the event, of not having done *nearly* enough.

If you race infrequently—once, twice, or three times a summer—there's little to gain by *not* tapering, since your primary motivation is to come away from the race with good thoughts in your head. Be careful, though; athletes at all levels have been known to use their taper as an excuse not to do anything at all. Under cover of gearing up, they eat like crazy in front of the television set for a week, put on 10 pounds, then race poorly—worse than if they'd trained hard right up until race day. If you need that kind of excuse *not* to train, perhaps your program is too ambitious for your lifestyle. Backing off on your training intensity and mileage should make you eager to race and anxious to get back up to 100 percent.

In my own program, I put much less emphasis on tapering than I did a few years ago, primarily because my program itself is geared to decreasing the need for long periods of recovery between long, intense workouts. In other words, the years of endurance training have given me just what they were supposed to have given me: endurance. Stay with this sport long enough, and you'll find the same thing happening to you.

Generally, for the short- and medium-distance races during the season that are a part of my training routine, I back off the day before the race. I might not swim, and I'll take just a light run and a short, easy ride. I'm not even training, really; I'm just keeping things loose.

For more important races, I'll go easy for two or three days, with very little at all the day before the event.

For you, experimentation is the only way. Even if you don't keep a strict training log, maintain some record of the two-week period prior to your races. Once you've gotten six or seven events under your belt, take a look at what worked and what didn't. But even if you see a pattern and are able to come up with a plan of attack, be prepared to watch it crumble for no reason that you can rationally ascertain. Good days and bad days are a part of this sport that may never be fully understood.

Nutrition

Nothing, not even tapering, is as personal or mysterious as prerace nutrition. Medical theories on the subject are out of date almost before they are published. Two general schools of thought, however, seem to be generally accepted:

1. The best thing to eat is what you've been eating during your training. Racing in a triathlon is pushing your body pretty far as it is. Why complicate things by adding to the stress with new and unfamiliar food?

2. The most critical day is two days before the race, not the day before. If you're participating in a half- or full-Ironman-distance event, eat *slightly* more than you usually do on the Friday before a Sunday race, then eat slightly less than you normally do on Saturday.

Pay a lot of attention to staying hydrated.

Current thinking that I personally agree with suggests that whatever you eat should be in the form of complex carbohydrates: fruit, bread, and pasta are good.

Common sense, moderation, and experience are your best teachers here. If you're hoping to find a magic formula the night before a race that's going to turn you into Superman, forget it. Experiment with your prerace diet during the months of training, then stick with what has worked for you. Perhaps even better, stay away from what *hasn't* worked.

Hydration

Pay a lot of attention to this one, even when all you've got in front of you is a short distance race. Heat and dehydration will stop you more quickly than any other factor in a triathlon. Prehydration, beginning a couple of days before the event, is a must. The common guideline is to drink until your urine runs frequently and clear. By no means drink only when you're thirsty the day before a triathlon, especially if the weather is expected to be warm.

Dr. Mac Larsen, a San Diego-based physician who is himself a longtime runner and triathlete, recommends at least eight eight-ounce glasses of water during the two days prior to a triathlon, assuming you're on a taper and not training.

"If you're still training during those two days," says Larsen, "it's an entirely different ball game. You can quadruple that figure and still come up short. The clear urine test is your best basic guideline."

Larsen also recommends a relatively salty last meal before a race, followed by several glasses of water. "You may feel a little soggy after a meal like that," he says, "but that feeling will wear off soon after the race begins. A salty meal will help your body retain fluids taken the day before the race. Avoid alcohol, which can have a dehydrating effect, and, if you're a race-day coffee drinker, drink it as close to the starting time as your stomach will allow. That way you'll benefit from the positive aspects of caffeine—the increased potential for fatty acid metabolism, for example—and not suffer from its diuretic effect."

RACE DAY

The more experienced you get, the more you're tempted to believe you've got the routine licked and the closer you feel you can shave the time between your arrival at the race site and the starting gun. In fact, the exact opposite is true. If anything, I've become pickier over the years about my prerace ritual.

I'm in the transition area setting up my bike at least two hours before the start of a race, and it often feels like there's still not enough time. My advice is to beat the crowds—check in, get your arms and legs marked, then set up your transition area early. That will give you plenty of time to warm up, scout out the area, and then double-check before the gun.

Using a formal checklist when you're setting up your transition area is a good idea. Concentrate on duplicating the routine you've used before, or, if it's your first race, go slowly and carefully. Then, when everything is ready—when your bike is racked, your shoes and clothing are laid out—take a step back and look over the entire area. Find out which way you'll be coming into the transition area from the swim, which way you'll be heading out on the bike, and so on. The idea is to make all of your moves during the race itself as close to second nature as possible. By being totally familiar with your personal corner of the triathlon world, you'll decrease the chances of the little things going wrong that are eventually going to go wrong no matter *what* you do.

Warming Up

Many people think that, because they're doing a triathlon, a warm-up is unnecessary. It's funny that in a sport populated by overdoers I've been accused of being a fanatic by other triathletes who see me warming up before an event: "Not gonna be enough for you today, Tinley?"

But warming up before a triathlon of any distance is a good idea. If you go into the race cold, chances are it's going to take you a long time and a lot of heavy breathing to get up to full steam. Think about it: how many times have you jumped right into a workout and blasted away at 100 percent effort right from the start? And what have you felt like when you've tried? A slow, easy warm-up

Stretch and get a good warm-up before your races. If you go in cold, it's going to take a lot of energy just to get all the parts of your body up to steam.

on race day will let you go hard right from the gun. Your race will be faster and probably a lot more enjoyable.

About an hour and 15 minutes before the start of a race, I go for a short run—no more than a mile to a mile-and-a-half. Then I stretch for 10 or 15 minutes. After that, I get on the bike and ride for 15 minutes—not hard, but enough so that my legs get a little bit of work before I swim. How important is this part of your warm-up? Well, because his bike on Ironman race morning is secured in the highly guarded transition area, Dave Scott has actually brought a spare bike to Hawaii for his prerace warm-up.

I'd recommend warming up for the swim too, unless the water is very cold. One of the biggest problems beginning triathletes have is hyperventilation when they find themselves in the middle of a mass swim start. Fear is part of the reaction, but so is the shock of the cold water and the simple exhaustion of suddenly taxed muscles that don't have enough blood in them to work properly. Unless conditions are severe, give your mind and your upper body a taste of what's to come before the gun goes off. Also use the warm-up to sight landmarks behind the marked bouys so that you'll be able to navigate efficiently.

The Swim

The wave swim starts that were first used in the 1984 Bud Light U.S. Triathlon Series have revolutionized this area of the sport. No longer was it necessary for 1,000 athletes to rush *en masse* into the water, clawing and kicking. But there are still plenty of big races that don't use the wave starts, and, even with the waves, a tightly bunched group of 200 swimmers is no picnic.

Self-seeding is a must, and it works to everyone's advantage. If you're slow and you start in front, the athletes behind you are going to have to take the time to swim rudely over your broken body. Nobody wins.

If you're not sure about your ability as a swimmer, ease into the middle of the pack, keep your eyes open and your wits about you, and take advantage of the tremendous draft.

Drafting can make a big difference in your swim, although it's not as effective (or as illegal) as drafting on the bike. (Figures show that drafting on the swim can give you a 5–7 percent advantage, while on the bike it can make up to a 25 percent difference.) The best method is to swim directly behind or slightly to the left or right of the person in front of you. You know you're close enough when you are surrounded by the bubbles caused by his or her kick. This can be disconcerting if you haven't tried it before, but the technique can be mastered quickly. A great time to practice is during pool workouts. Move into a lane where the swimmers are normally faster than you are and latch on.

There are two dangers in drafting. First, swimmers have been known to object to their toes being nicked by another swimmer's fingers every few yards. Things can get nasty in a competitive situation, so don't stay *too* close for too long. Second, you're totally dependent on the person in front of you for navigation. If that swimmer is wrong, you're wrong, a lesson I've learned the hard way several times.

**"Racing" is for everyone.
Pick out riders in front of you and then
catch them one at a time.**

The Bike

Take it easy during the first few minutes of your bike ride; it's likely that you're a lot more wobbly than you think after spending 20 minutes to an hour or more in the water, especially if the water was cold and your brain and legs need some time to get back into the swing of things. Spin your pedals in low gears for a mile or two and work gradually into the hard stuff. Understand that you probably won't feel great right off the bat. Concentrate on settling yourself into a good relaxed riding position before you worry about trying to pass people. Some good athletes never race as well as they train, simply because they never allow themselves that little bit of time to settle down and focus on the task at hand. A fine line exists between being too nervous and tense and being totally laid-back and uncaring. It's great to have that good rush of adrenaline to get you going, but, if you can't control it, you'll make too many mistakes.

I use the first miles of the bike ride to assess my position in the race and decide what my strategy will be. Since most of the athletes I'm concerned with are better swimmers than I am, there's almost never a choice: I'm going to be riding as fast and as hard as possible. Your individual strategy, however, may hinge on a couple of factors.

A good understanding of your own abilities along with a knowledge of the course and weather conditions really helps in planning your race. Is it a hilly course, and, if so, should you take advantage of your strong hill-climbing abilities and ride extra-hard? Or perhaps the water was very cold on the swim and it looks as if you feel better on the bike than everyone around you. The thing to do in that case would be to go hard and make the most of the temporary advantage.

At the 1985 Bud Light USTS race in Chicago, many people were surprised when Scott Molina was still in third place behind his brother Sean and Charlie Graves at the turnaround at the north end of the course. Once the turn was made, though, Molina was quick to pass his brother and overtake Graves. Why? Scott said later that he figured that riding hard into the headwind he'd felt on the way north would have been counterproductive, since the harder he pushed, the more the wind was going to push back. He decided to conserve his energy and make a strong move only when the wind was finally at his back. The strategy worked—neither Mark Allen nor I could catch him on the run. He won the race by almost a full minute.

Remember that "racing" a triathlon is not just for the professionals and the top age-groupers. As you settle into your ride, pick out specific athletes in front of you and try to catch them as you go. Or note carefully the cyclists who pass you early in the race who seem to be working extra hard. Is there a chance that you will catch them once again later in the race? Since I'm coming from behind on the bike, I play a little Pac-Man game in my mind, gobbling up riders as I go and gaining energy from each one.

Probably more than anything, riding the bike with the knowledge that it's only part of the triathlon is a big help. Especially in long races, but even in short ones, you'll constantly bounce back and forth from high points to low points. Relax, assess your own physical condition continuously, and race your own race.

**Joanne Ernst works hard on the toughest transition:
off the bike and into the run.**

The Run

Over the last few miles of the bike course, start thinking about your run: how you're going to come into the transition area, where your stuff is, what clothing or equipment you're going to take off or put on. Don't go overboard, though, especially on a bike course that is fairly technical or confusing, because you need to get into the transition area before you can start running. In a major race in Los Angeles in 1985, a triathlete stayed with me on the bike through the whole 25-mile course. He was a great rider; I still don't know who he was. Two miles from the finish line, he missed a really obvious turn, and I never saw him again. He just wasn't paying attention.

During the last half-mile, go through some of the stretching and loosening up routines described under "Tranistion Tips" in Chapter 2. Generally, you should get your body into a different position from the one it's been in during the bike ride. Again, though, be aware of where you are and what you're doing—don't ruin your race and someone else's by crashing into a runner during an elaborate on-the-bike calisthenic routine.

As you start the run, don't panic at how terrible your legs feel at first. Things will get better. And by no means let the excitement of the transition area—the noise of the crowd, your wife or your girlfriend or boyfriend cheering for you—turn you into an instant hero. Trying to look strong and fast in the transition area is a great way to end up with cramps and worse. Pacing is important, and so is having the maturity to apply it intelligently. Unless you're one of the fortunate few who can blast off the bike and fly, you should ease into your run. It'll save you a long walk back from the turnaround.

Keep in mind that your running ability alone sometimes has very little to do with how well you can run after cycling. In mid-1985, in her second year in the sport, New Zealander Allison Roe, the former world record holder in the marathon, was still wondering why she couldn't run well in a triathlon after riding hard. "My back just *aches*," she said after a race in Los Angeles. While part of her problem was undoubtedly a poorly adjusted bicycle, her complaint makes the point nicely.

Naturally, the bottom line in any race is what you get out of it. Merely finishing your first triathlon is a big thrill; getting technically and physically better as time goes on is just as rewarding. Keep your goals and your individual performances in perspective, however. I think you should always finish a race thinking that you could have gone just a little bit faster. It leaves you a little something for next time. I hate to see people finish a race and just pass out or start getting sick along the side of the road. First, I don't think that's very healthy, and second, I don't think it does the sport any good from an image standpoint.

Unless you're racing for all the marbles (and probably not even then), pushing yourself to 110 percent—to the edge of collapse—doesn't make a whole lot of sense. Not even the best athletes in the world lay everything on the line every time they go out. Challenge yourself when you race, sure, but be aware of the total picture as you do. The real point of this whole thing for 99 percent of the people involved is maintaining a healthy, superfit lifestyle. Recovering from one grueling, gut-wrenching ordeal after another hardly serves that purpose.

"The conditions were extreme, and I wanted to go above and beyond. I wanted a chance to prove that I'm the faster runner—that when it comes down to a footrace I'm a competitor."—Dave Scott after the 1984 Ironman Triathlon

8
IT'S ALL IN THE MIND

At the Cascade Lake Triathlon in Bend, Oregon, in August 1985, I came off the bike with a good lead, but I was feeling terrible as I moved through the first half of the 13-mile run course. It had been a long day, with a cold swim and a tough, hilly bike ride. Now it was hot, and the logging trail I was on was dusty from cars and camera trucks and volunteers at the aid stations. I was dying on the gradual uphill.

At about the six-mile mark, the road turned into a narrow trail, which at times was hard to follow because it was so unused. Suddenly there were no people, the vehicles couldn't follow, and I was alone. Enclosed in the forest, I could see the lake sparkling through the trees. There wasn't a sound except the soft crunch of my shoes on the trail and my own breathing. It was beautiful. While a quarter-mile before I had been struggling, I floated now, content with the obvious strategy: to relax and enjoy the racing, to go as well and as hard as I could. If someone came from behind, then I'd have enough to stay with him. Or I wouldn't. In any case, I'd know I'd done all I could do.

The end result was that my pace picked up almost a minute a mile, and I ended up winning the race with plenty of room to spare. Nothing really magical had happened, except that I had stopped worrying and started running. The trees and the lake had merely been the catalysts that jogged my mind into the proper framework.

I think you can talk yourself into, or out of, almost anything. Triathletes are especially good at both, and they can swing from one extreme to another several times during a race. There are physical fears to conquer, like heavy surf and cold ocean water or a fast downhill turn on the bike (or dusty roads), and mental

Think positively!

mountains of endurance to climb as well. The winners, sometimes just the finishers, are those who are able to maintain the necessary level of confidence, composure, and concentration from start to finish. There is no place for self-doubt in a triathlon, yet self-doubt runs rampant through the ranks of even the best. It's a problem that strong arms and legs are only partially capable of solving.

CONFIDENCE

Knowing you can accomplish a goal—being reasonably sure of success, at least—bounces right back into your training program. No level of positive thinking is going to get you through even a two- or three-hour event in good shape if you haven't run a step in a year. You might *finish*, but you'll probably hate yourself for trying, and what's the point in that?

Remember the goals I talked about in Chapter 6. Set your mind on achieving them and be careful to examine your motivation along the way. Getting there should be much more than half the fun. If you're miserable over the thought of having to train, but scared to death over the thought of the race day that's fast approaching, it's time for a reanalysis of your program.

Getting to the Finish Line in One Piece

Having gone the distance before is a big, big confidence builder. That's why your second triathlon is always easier mentally than your first (although it's often tougher physically because you've gotten cocky). With unknowns in front of it, your mind tends to create barriers, so remove as many of those unknowns as possible. I'm not suggesting that you go out and do a practice Ironman a month before your flight leaves for Hawaii, but entering a marathon or two in the months prior to race day wouldn't be a bad idea at all. Don't race them; just go the distance as part of your training program. Completing them successfully will help both physically and mentally. And if you have trouble—if you go out too hard, or don't take enough water, or find that you're wearing the wrong shoes— you've learned valuable lessons and made the mistakes when you could afford to make them. When the day for your Ironman does come, you'll have an idea at least of what you're up against.

If your goal is a shorter race—even one as long as a half-Ironman-distance event—take a weekend day well before the race (six weeks out at least) and go the distance. Swim early in the morning, then eat breakfast and relax for a while, then get on the bike. Ride smoothly and don't push. Stretch well when you're finished, rehydrate yourself, stretch again, then head out *slowly* into your run. Take all the time you need; walk if you have to—just get through the distance so that you'll have a reference point on race day. You'll be able to stand at the starting line, confident of the most important point of all: Yes, I can finish.

If you can train on the actual course of the event, all the better. Once again,

Dave Scott heads out of the transition area at the 1984 Ironman with fire in his eyes, despite being nine minutes behind Mark Allen. Everyone had said it: Allen would have to fall down for Scott to win. When Allen fell, Dave was right there.

Sometimes, all the best planning in the world simply goes to prove how even things can be. Scott Molina and I tied for first at the Atlanta Bud Light US Triathlon Series race in 1984.

it's a case of removing as many unknowns as possible so that your mind won't be able to play little confidence-destroying games with itself. Terry Cotten, a top road runner out of San Diego, once said that he trained on a course of an important race as often as possible, "because every time I run it, it gets a little bit shorter."

Whether you've gone the distance before or not, there comes a time when there's no more you can do. On race morning you must complete the training process by forming your strategy along the guidelines your training has provided. Don't be an idiot and surge to the front of the pack when you know you're going to get pounded by the faster swimmers after the first 50 yards. But don't shrink to the back automatically, either. Be sure of your ability level within a reasonable spectrum, then ignore the gremlins that whisper that you should have done this or that. Make yourself believe that you're ready, because if you *can't*, then you're *not*. "The feeling I get at the starting line," Julie Moss once said, "is that it's over—all the hard work and the training are over. The race is the fun part."

Something I find helpful is going over the logistics of the race step by step in my mind before the start. I think about the transition area, what the course is like, what the traffic flow of cyclists and runners is, so that I could almost do the race blindfolded. Having my mind settled in that one area makes it much easier to be confident in others.

Confidence can also be fortified by breaking your race into sections that offer less of a challenge than the race as a whole. If you come from a running background, the idea of covering 40 miles in three hours of competition can be frightening. So don't think about that. Get to the first buoy on the swim, *then* think about getting to number two. Ride to the turnaround of the bike course before you start thinking about the trip back. Tackle the run course mile by mile, not as a 6- or 10-mile ordeal. Handle the pieces one at a time until the only piece left swings the door to the finish line wide open. "There were only nine miles to go on the run after I got to the turnaround at the airport," said Kathleen McCartney about her marathon the year she won the Ironman. "That was the distance of my run through the Back Bay in Newport Beach. I knew I could do that!"

Racing

There is another dimension to confidence when a triathlete moves beyond just finishing and into racing. There are chances to be taken, perhaps a pace to run or bike or swim that you might not be entirely confident of being able to hold. In that case, you must have enough faith in your own judgment and ability to go beyond previously established limits. How far beyond and at what point in the race you go depends on you, but the decision should be based in reality. If you've never run a 10K in less than 35 minutes, but you head out of the transition area at a 5-minute-per-mile pace, that's ignorance, not confidence.

An important point, though, about pressing your limits in competition against athletes who are a level or two above you: it's a heck of a way to improve. Your idea of fast is not the same as *their* idea of fast, and sometimes the difference is merely in the doing.

There's a fine line between racing your own race and testing yourself against

Kathleen McCartney:
"There were only nine miles to go at
the turnaround. I *knew* I could run that!"

the guy pedaling past you. I suggested earlier that the triathletes who just wanted to finish an event should let him go. I'll suggest that if you want to *race*—if you want to improve—you might want to stay with him. If you're cycling, don't draft. Let him move up 20 yards or so, then put your head down and go. Keep your mind on what your own body is doing, but look up every so often to gauge the distance. If he's gaining, push harder. Test yourself until you reach the point where going farther is going to hurt your performance. You may have to drop off. Then again, you may not. You'll never know unless you give it a try. The greatest part about testing the limits is that, once you reach a new plateau, you'll usually stay there.

COMPOSURE

There is little need for the explosive, frantic energy of a sprinter in the sport of triathlon, where even short races take the average athlete two and a half hours. Patience is surely a virtue in triathloning, but, more than that, staying in control of your mind and your body is critical. While seconds lost in a transition area are difficult to regain, energy lost in mental disorganization and confusion is irreplaceable.

The best example I know that illustrates the value of keeping your head in the

Jacqueline Shaw raced superbly at the World's Toughest Triathlon in Lake Tahoe in 1984. She crossed the finish line first with a 34-minute lead. But she had ignored race rules, running a stop light on the bike course. The resulting disqualification cost her $10,000. Keep your mind working along with your body during a race.

right place is that of Jacqueline Shaw at the World's Toughest Triathlon in Lake Tahoe on September 8, 1984. On the mountainous 120-mile bike course, Shaw, a Canadian living in Del Mar, California, had a big lead over second-place Angela French of Phoenix, Arizona. Impatient and aggressive in the heat of the competition and afraid to give up even a few precious seconds, Shaw ran a red light at an intersection despite a stern prerace warning that such an action would mean automatic disqualification. "It'll be green in a minute," Shaw called over her shoulder to a race official as she rode off. Unfortunately, by the time it did, the official had already taken down her number. Shaw went on to finish first among the women in the event—by a full 34 minutes—but her effort came to nothing when the rule about the traffic regulations was enforced. She was disqualified and was not only bumped from the final results, but from the awards list, too. First prize went to French instead: $10,000 in crisp $100 bills.

Not all of us must learn the lesson as harshly as Jacqueline Shaw, but the price of losing one's sense of perspective in competition is often steep. At best, being frantic and out of control is exhausting, mentally and physically. At worst, it's the cause of mistakes that can be dangerous.

Looking at the Event Before You Race

Some of the most effective techniques used by sports psychologists to enhance the performance of their patients revolve around relaxation techniques. An athlete is taught (and relaxation under pressure is definitely something that must be learned) to examine and reexamine his or her body at regular intervals for areas of tension buildup. Where it exists, circulation can be impaired and oxygen exchange in the muscles or lungs hindered. The most graphic example of this in triathletes is panic and hyperventilation during mass swim starts. It's easy to get caught up in the desperate kicking and clawing. By the time you get to the first buoy, you're exhausted.

Probably the best way to combat panic and disorientation—to ensure that your competitive effort is contained within a framework of composure—is to allow some time for yourself before the race to relax and go through the event piece by piece in your mind.

What you'll actually be doing is using a subtle form of self-hypnosis or meditation. Sit away from the crowd after all your prerace logistics have been taken care of. Close your eyes and simply relax for a minute or two. Let your mind wander so that you can get a feel for the specific things that are bothering you. You'll pick up a lot of holes in your operation this way—the chin strap on your helmet that should be loosened, the spare bathing cap you meant to bring that's still in the car. Once you've dealt with all that junk and your mind is quiet, take yourself through the race and plan around areas that have presented problems in the past. *Plan* on being calm in the swim. *Plan* on breathing deeply before the start and not pushing hard until you've reached the first buoy. Bring yourself into the transition area and off your bike mentally; start the run in your mind fully equipped, with your shoes tied and your number on the front of your shirt. Most important, force yourself to see the race as a whole, from start to

I get fierce during a race.

finish, so that you're not going to blow the whole day by cranking yourself into the ground on the bike and having to crawl back to the finish line on the run.

The point is to calm yourself (you'll hear some people use the phrase *center yourself*) in preparation for an event completed within the guidelines that *you* set, not those set for you by the frenzy of other competitors, the conditions, or whatever.

Staying Calm Even When Nobody Else Is

Mental preparation can be maximized once the race has begun if you make a point of frequently reexamining your mind and body during the competition. The best times to do this are at pivotal junctures you may have identified before the starting gun. If you've planned on going hard in the swim after you've reached the first buoy, then refocus your efforts at that point, assess your condition, then let your body gradually move into high gear. If you've just taken off on the bike and there are riders and spectators all around you, work hard to stay within yourself. Compose yourself mentally and physically for the effort ahead. Bounce away from a situation that wants to control you and back to the state of mind you were in before the start of the event.

"I do a lot of visualization before a race," Mark Allen says. "I picture in my mind how I want to feel in a race. When I reach a point during the event where I start to hurt and want to back off, for example, the way I *want* to feel starts running through my mind. If I just keep repeating that, it can pull me back into feeling good."

CONCENTRATION

Rich Brownsberger, an excellent runner from San Diego who competed for UCLA, once said that he'd never been in a road race where he didn't feel like he wanted to quit. "It *hurts*," he said, "so in a 10K, for instance, I concentrate on getting to the next mile mark. I tell myself that I'll stop when I get there. When I do, I talk myself into going on to the next one, *then* stopping. Finally I get to five, and I figure I may as well finish; there's only one more mile to go."

You can deal with competition in many different ways, but deal with it you must. We all suffer mental and physical highs and lows. We all get bored once

Julie Leach's problem at the Horny Toad Triathlon in San Diego in 1982? Gain back 13 minutes on a 13-mile run.

in a while during long races. We all feel hurt and doubt our own physical abilities. Concentration is the key to being able to cope, although finding the *method* of concentration that works for you is the tough part.

Your mental approach to competition is, by and large, a function of your competitive goals, so it's important to have those clear in your mind before the gun goes off. If it's your first race, then your mental strategy should focus on getting you to the finish line. Thoughts of how everyone else in the event is doing should be put firmly aside. If you're racing to win—either overall or within an age group—then you always must be conscious of your position relative to the

**Scott Molina,
"The Terminator,"
concentrates on first place.**

athletes you want to beat. In a third case, you may be looking merely to perform better than you ever have, regardless of how you place. An entirely different mental framework may then be necessary.

Confronting Reality

I tend to focus more on what's in front of me—more on the race itself—than on something internal. There are athletes who use visualization techniques, mantras, and a wide variety of mental games to maximize their performance. Personally, I would side with a guy like Brownsberger, who confronts the harsh reality of his effort head-on.

To me, a triathlon is a technical and physical challenge. I want to get from one place to another as quickly as possible, passing as many people as I can along the way. That I think this way is hardly surprising since I've never been among the leaders coming out of the swim. Getting to the front has always involved a lot of simple hard work. I think that if I spent a greater portion of my races in first place—alone with only myself to deal with—I would probably end up relying on more exotic methods to keep my level of effort where it needs to be.

When you race against other people, you must do so armed with a healthy dose of what we talked about in the beginning of this chapter: confidence. It also helps to be particularly strong in one or two events. When I come out of the water with ground to make up, I *know* I'm going to be able to do so on the bike, and my experience tells me that I'll make up even more on the run. That makes an outwardly competitive game plan feasible. On the other hand, if you're a great swimmer, but only a fair cyclist and a slow runner, concentrating on your performance relative to those around you during the last two-thirds of a race is going to be awfully depressing.

Coming from behind involves a certain level of aggression that I think is indispensable. I get fierce during a race, almost angry at times, and, as long as that feeling can be well directed, it is a valuable tool. Where many athletes go wrong is in allowing their aggression to leak into extraneous areas. They get angry with the course, the volunteers, their bike. Instead of helping them, their competitive nature keeps their mind off the basic issue.

Concentrating on the race, moving toward the front, my mind is occupied with the hundreds of tiny details that go along with racing. Boredom, especially in the shorter races, is impossible. On the bike: Am I spinning the pedals and lifting my knees the way I want? Is my body position good? Are my hands relaxed on the brake hoods? Am I pushing the right gear? On the run: Am I going out too hard? Am I catching the guy in front? Is my upper body relaxed?

Dealing with specifics like this keeps my mind focused on what I'm doing and where I need to be going. It also prepares me to make quick decisions when the situation warrants it. In short races especially, where the pace is furious throughout, taking corners at high speeds, watching for course markings, hitting the gears correctly for short, steep climbs are critical points that must get your undivided attention. You can mantra yourself right into a tree if you get too wrapped up in mystical solutions to concrete problems.

Mark Allen.

Disassociation

Even when I'm concentrating well in a race, I often find myself fighting a battle to stave off thoughts that have nothing to do with the event. I can never figure out what yesterday morning's breakfast has to do with the top of a hill I just climbed or how the new shirt that's sitting at home in the closet connects with the aid station 100 yards up the road. Every competitor is familiar with this kind of experience; the athletes who are the most successful at refocusing their minds are the ones who succeed.

In longer races—half-Ironman and beyond—I think you can afford yourself a bit of diversion. It takes you out of the present and away from the pain, and that's a real blessing at times. The longer you're away from the race, though, the harder it is to get back.

I'm convinced that your performance slacks off when you're thinking about something else. There's a little extra edge between pedaling 21½ miles an hour and pedaling 22. That half-mile-per-hour difference comes from something inside that you have to dig for, but you can reach it only if you focus. Allowing yourself to drift away from the reality of your effort may make you feel better, but it makes you less effective as a competitor, too.

The flip side of the coin is the use of disassociation techniques geared toward increasing your work load. Rather than shrink from pain and intensity by removing themselves from the situation mentally, some athletes attack their fatigue and their doubts with a wide array of psychological weapons. No one I know has verbalized his use of this kind of mind-gaming better than Mark Allen.

"I remember racing in the Tampa Bud Light USTS," he said in the fall of 1984 after he'd won a whole series of races by wide margins. "I felt in control of everything, especially on the bike. I just put my head down and concentrated. The whole time, all I looked at was my chain ring going around. It really made me focus on what I was doing. When I started to get just a little burned out, I'd shift right away, and once I got a little bit rested, I'd shift back up and start pushing it again.

"You've got a physical limit beyond which you can't go any harder for more than a mile or two—a definite point on the edge of your capability. I try to bounce off that point when I'm racing well—just getting to the edge of where I have to back off, then holding it there. The natural inclination of your body is to slow down, so I have to keep pushing myself back to that point."

Disassociation can certainly be a big help in getting you out of a specific competitive rut. My experience at the Cascade Lake Triathlon, described at the beginning of the chapter, illustrates that point well. The woods and the sudden serenity took my mind off the race just for a moment, but long enough for my mind to rethink the problem. All I needed to do was relax.

Other athletes are more deliberate with their imagery. A technique many people use is to call up a visual image of a runner or a swimmer or a cyclist that they admire. It might be, for instance, Sebastian Coe winning a mile or Bernard Hinault climbing through the Alps in the Tour de France. When things get tough, it's possible to dig yourself out of a hole by ignoring your own situation and calling up that competitive ideal, then easing your own body into the pattern.

Disassociation can also help in long races, where boredom can be as crushing an enemy as the heat or the distance. In races like the Ironman in Hawaii, fairly sophisticated forms of self-hypnosis have been used with great success. Allen stares at his chain ring endlessly, until everything and everyone around him is a blur; other athletes ride the white line or lock their attention onto the front wheel of their bicycle; they watch their knees move up and down or listen to the exaggerated sound of their own breathing. Whatever technique you use, you should bounce back into the real world frequently enough to keep your performance level where you want it.

Pain Management

Everybody who competes in endurance competition hurts. How should you deal with it? Tom Warren wonders at the normal reaction: "Why should I automatically slow down when I feel bad? Maybe *speeding up* will make me feel better!"

Maybe it will. The point is that the pain of the triathlete (and I'm assuming here that we're not talking about the sharp, persistent pain of injury) is not the same red-line pain of the 400-meter track star. His problem is the limited ability of the human body to function anaerobically. A triathlete, on the other hand, hurts over the long haul, from aerobic fatigue, so his or her breaking point is more flexible. In almost every case, it's the mind that cracks before the legs or the lungs do.

That some triathletes deal better with pain than others is obvious. They can push their bodies harder than most. There are even medical studies dealing with by-products of muscle breakdown in the blood that offer scientific evidence of this. *How* they do it, though, is the question.

Go inside yourself when it hurts— sometimes you can think your way through the tough spots.

One answer is that they've learned how to handle pain in training. Certainly, that's one of the benefits I derive from my high-intensity workouts. I condition myself to run faster for longer periods of time, and with every 400-yard interval I do I become more familiar with the level of discomfort I can suffer and still move on. When I'm confronted with the same situation in competition, when I need not only the speed but also the knowledge that I can hang on for one mile or two or three, then stopping the pain becomes less urgent because I've been there before and survived.

Experiment by increasing your maximum level of intensity (and, therefore, pain) in both your racing and your training. Ease yourself over the edge of safety once in a while, like a turtle poking its head out of its shell. Do it bit by bit, testing the environment for danger as you go. What you'll probably find is that the higher levels of performance you thought were restricted by physical limitations are instead functions of your own mind and its ability to deal with your being uncomfortable.

"What training does," said Mark Allen, "is enable you to be comfortable with pain—with the feeling of your body wanting to stop but your mind pushing you through that. The more you get accustomed to being in that situation in your training, the less foreign it will be when you race. You're able to push all the way to the finish line because you know you've done it before, and you've recovered. I think that's the biggest fear: that the pain will be so bad that it's never going to go away. It always does, though. Ten or 15 minutes after the race, it's always gone."

"Oh, my God, look at all the *bodies*!"—female spectator in the transition area of the 1985 Bud Light U.S. Triathlon Series National Championship

9
TRIATHLON CLOTHING AND EQUIPMENT

The technical complexity of the sport of triathlon is one of its greatest attractions. People outside the sport are amazed at the flash and the glitter of the spectacle: the colorful Lycra, the brightly painted bicycles sparkling with chrome, the ease with which the competitors deal with moving from one activity to another without so much as a blink. John Daley, an operations producer for ESPN, the all-sports cable network, saw his first triathlon at the Bud Light U.S. Triathlon Series National Championships at Hilton Head Island, South Carolina, in 1985 and was suitably impressed:

"I was really surprised," he said. "When the first guy came out of the water, I thought he was going to take his time, change into his cycling shorts, take off his helmet, change shoes, and then head out. I turned to look for the next swimmer, and when I turned back he was gone. I had to watch the next guys to figure out what had happened. I mean, they came in and went out: zoom! They really knew what they were doing."

The competitors, especially the newly converted, are eager to jump right in. A newcomer usually sees him- or herself as a kind of high-tech Barbie doll. No fashion is too new, no piece of equipment is too expensive, no accessory is too trivial. In contrast to the folks who populated the running boom, triathletes have a reputation for being outgoing, gregarious, and eager to explore new ground—and their clothing reflects this.

It's not hard to see why this is so. Triathletes interested in being "totally fit" are naturally going to be conscious of how they look. They want to dress in clothing and buy equipment that will enhance their appearance, and if there's more than just a little narcissism wrapped up in all of this, what's the harm?

Personally, I'm all for it. The gadgetry and the high-tech aspect of the sport are fun for a lot of us. And, as far as the clothing goes, well, *feeling* fast and racy on the road often has plenty to do with *being* fast and racy.

Here's a brief, sport-by-sport view of what you'll need and how to make it work for you.

THE SWIM

Suit

If you've raced before, you have many suits; if you haven't, your first brief, nylon or Lycra racing suit is going to be an experience. Wearing it in public is going to be worse. The best plan is to wear it only in the company of other triathletes whose bodies and outward demeanor will inspire admiration and not derisive taunts from the local citizenry.

The fact is that you can get by without a racing suit if your only intent is an informal, local triathlon, but the aqua-dynamic and fast-drying properties of competition suits make them a must for training and racing.

Goggles

This is another must for most swimmers except the toughest of oceangoing die-hards. If you train in chlorinated water and you plan to keep your first pair of

The trisuit.

eyeballs longer than a few years, you'll search long and hard for a pair of goggles that fits well and doesn't leak; such goggles will become a trusted friend.

Actually, one of the reasons goggles were first used was to help competitive swimmers see their arms and thus improve their strokes, so there are more benefits to them than just comfort. There are many different styles on the market, made by several different manufacturers. Find a style that works for you and buy a bunch of them before they are replaced by a new and improved model that won't work at all.

Swim Cap

For pool training, the thin, elastic kind are good and will keep the person who cuts your hair happy. (He or she would be happier still if you stopped swimming in chlorinated water altogether.)

Caps keep your head warm and streamlined. For racing in cold water, wear two, or buy a neoprene hood. Hoods were originally made for scuba divers and surfers, but now are available specifically for triathletes. Since the head and neck area accounts for much of your body heat loss during a cold-water swim, a good cap can make a big difference in your performance.

Swim Fins, Pull Buoys, Kickboards, Hand Paddles

Obviously for training only, these aids isolate parts of the body for specific training routines, add resistance, or force you into technically correct positions. Fins are great for developing leg and ankle strength along with ankle flexibility, a major factor in kicking efficiency. Watch out for knee pain when you train with fins—it's a sign of impending stress injury.

Paddles can make you strong and can correct poor hand position on your stroke. In fact, they're impossible to use if your hand is *not* positioned correctly. As with fins, though, be careful—if you feel shoulder pain after or during paddle use, stop or at least lighten up on the intensity.

Wet Suits

From the simple surfing vest to a full suit, wet suits can be critical in cold-water races. There are even some events—the World's Toughest Triathlon in Lake Tahoe is one of them—that *require* participants to use them. In a wet suit, you give up mobility and streamlining but gain buoyancy, then lose plenty of time in the transition area dragging the thing off—especially if only some of the competitors are wearing them.

If you race frequently, buy a vest, at least, and make it a part of your normal race kit. I was pulled out of the water with hypothermia in a race in Australia in 1985, and since then I usually carry along a suit if there's even the slightest thought in my mind that the water might be very cold. The implied rule here is that you should never take a race director's word for how warm the water is, how warm it's going to be, or how warm it was "last year."

THE BIKE

Bike and Components

Talk about basic. Yes, you will need a bicycle to do triathlons. My trying to explain what *kind* within the present context is ridiculous. Entire books have been written about just buying a bicycle, so all we'll say here is that for triathlons you should be looking for a time-trial bike (there are road-racing bikes and track bikes and touring bikes with frame characteristics specific to each task) with a stiff frame that is as light as possible. Read a couple of books on the subject, then head for a reputable bicycle shop.

Wheels

It's possible to upgrade a medium-priced bike tenfold by adding a good pair of wheels. Wheels should be light and durable, although for general triathlon use exotic, superlightweight wheels are probably counterproductive. One set of railroad tracks at the bottom of a bumpy downhill during a triathlon can put a big dent in both your pocketbook and your head. Stick to the basics until you become knowledgeable enough to look for something specifically suited to your expanded needs.

Tires

Once again, the decision is between the exotic and the practical: the lighter the tire, the faster you go; the lighter the tire, the more flats you get—and flats are about the best way I know of to slow down in a race. Also, lightweight racing tires are *very* expensive and cannot be fixed once you put a hole in one, so they are meant *only* for racing.

A recommendation: train on clincher tires (the ones with the replaceable tubes that require a tire iron to get on and off) and race on sew-ups (the ones that get glued onto the rim, with the tube literally sewn inside the tire). Sew-ups (or *tubulars*) are less durable than clinchers and more expensive to use, but are usually lighter and can be changed more quickly under race conditions.

Aero helmets do actually work— they reportedly will shave 10 seconds per 40 kilometers off your bike time.

Shorts

The standard cycling shorts before triathlons came along were boring black, usually made of wool or cotton, with a chamois crotch. I really don't think it's too much to say that triathlon shoved the cycling garment industry into heavy use of synthetic fabrics and a wide variety of colors, the wilder the better.

The basic issue still holds, though. Your shorts should fit well and be comfortable. The long legs prevent chafing on the inside of the thigh, a critical need in training and in long races. One sure sign of a poorly made cycling short is when the legs creep up beyond the seat. Some triathletes prefer the chamois crotch, but a crotch lining of polypropylene is very popular. Aerodynamic, skintight Lycra/spandex is the most popular choice of fabric for the shorts themselves.

Jerseys

Triathletes train on the bicycle in everything from old T-shirts to authentic wool European cycling jerseys. Whatever works for you works, although if you haven't tried something with pockets in the back for food and odds and ends, you should. They're a big help. Also keep in mind that the less you wear, the less protection you have in case of a fall.

When you race, pay more attention to the aerodynamics of your jersey. Anything that flops around and catches air costs you time, regardless of your ability level. Fastest of all is bare skin—I seldom wear a shirt during short races in warm weather.

Generally, on the bike, I'd recommend you dress in layers. It's warmer when the weather is cold and easier to adjust as the day heats up. Whatever you do, don't underdress. Plan for the worst if the weather is threatening when you head out on a ride.

Dian Girard, a top pro from Austin, Texas, shows off a trisuit. Notice the number secured around her waist by an elastic ribbon. During the run, she'll turn it around so that the number faces the front for the finish of the race.

Tri-suits

If you haven't seen them, you really are new to the sport. They're one-piece, skintight suits, usually of brightly colored Lycra/spandex, designed for use in all three events of the triathlon. They're good in the transition areas because they're fast. They're bad because they get very hot on the run. Also, if they don't fit perfectly, they can cause drag and/or chafing in the water.

The growing trend among the top triathletes is simply to wear their swimsuits throughout the race, especially in short-distance events. That goes the speed factor of the tri-suit one better and eliminates the other two problems. Comfort-wise, it can be tough, though. I've designed a swimsuit for myself with a small polypropylene crotch pad that works nicely. Chafing is still a problem, but experience will show you where to smear on the petroleum jelly to prevent that. In longer races, I'd recommend that you take the time and change into clothing for each of the three events that will be as comfortable as possible.

Shoes, Toe Clips, and Straps

Always wear cleated cycling shoes. It's almost impossible to learn good spinning technique without pulling up properly on the pedals, and you can't do that if you're not securely strapped into your toe clips. If you're a novice and you don't feel comfortable with this, practice until you do on long flat roads or parking lots where there isn't much traffic.

Helmets

Vanity puts a lot of dents in the heads of triathletes. Wearing a helmet is not nearly as dashing as having the wind flying through your hair at 20 miles an hour, but it's a heck of a lot safer. A hard-shell helmet is a must. Before you become a convert the hard way, buy one and wear it, not merely in races in which a hard shell is required, but in training, too. Be prepared to spend $40 or more and look for a helmet that is well ventilated.

One definite advantage to hard-shell helmets is that they're aerodynamic. Elongated, teardrop-shaped helmets are commonly seen at races, and reportedly they can cut off up to 10 seconds of time per 40 kilometers of riding.

**Helmets are a pain,
but a broken head is worse.**

Gloves

Cycling gloves have leather palms—their most important feature, since your hands don't. They save a lot of wear and tear on your hands during normal riding and even more if you fall. I don't wear them when I race because they take too much time to put on and take off, but, if you prefer to do so, save time in the transition area by putting them on after you leave on the bike, then remove them either on the way in before the run or after you start running (tuck them into your shorts and carry them along).

THE RUN

Shoes

Once again, entire books have been written on this subject. The wide variety of running styles, body builds, training intensities, etc., makes any recommendation here about what shoe is right for you almost worthless. I can, however, pass along some suggestions that might make choosing a shoe more than just a complete trial-and-error process.

Since running-related injuries by far comprise the bulk of injuries to triathletes, protection is the first consideraton. You might *look* fast in the latest pair of three-ounce red, white, and gold Super-Whizzos, but what will you feel like running a 10K after 25 miles of hard cycling? Remember that much of your competitive running as a triathlete is going to come when you're already pretty beaten up. Your natural style may be altered; your knees might be wobbly after the first two events. If you have a hidden biomechanical weakness, a shoe with insufficent support or protection will find it.

Become familiar with *how* you run. Have a friend watch your style and examine the way you plant your foot. Do you excessively pronate (land or roll to the inside of your foot) or supinate (land or roll to the outside)? Do you strike with your heel or your toe? Are there specific injuries that you've suffered from in the past?

Armed with as much knowledge about yourself as you can gather, read the shoe surveys in the national magazines, then get to the local running store and ask some questions. A couple of things to keep in mind:

Don't Scrimp. An expensive shoe is not always the best shoe, but bargain shoes are always bad. The potential for injury is not worth the savings. When in doubt about shoe wear, buy another pair. Midsoles compress quickly, and, by the time you've put in 1,000 miles, they've lost 50 percent of their shock absorption capability. The outer sole may look fine, but for you, the triathlete, the shoe has worn out its usefulness.

Avoid Gimmicks. Some "high-tech" running shoes are a little like American cars in the late '50s: all flash, with a lot of chrome, big tail fins, and red plastic. There are some valuable things happening in running shoe research within the industry, but there are many features on shoes that represent little more than advances in mass marketing. Keep an eye out.

Clothing

The nicest thing about running is that you don't *need* a thing except two shoes and a pair of shorts. But there's a big difference between what you don't need and what you must have. Triathletes lead the way in the outrageous action-wear department. The current trend is toward wild patterns in natural fibers replacing the traditional nylon shorts, and a pair of tights as soon as there is just a touch of chill in the air is fashion-essential. The tights look good—they're sexy and streamlined—and they've become somewhat of a triathlete trademark because of their versatility (the same pair will keep you warm on the bike and on the run).

MISCELLANY

Sunglasses

During a long- or ultra-distance triathlon, sunglasses can be a big help. They cut the glare for safety, keep the bugs out of your eyes, and in both the bike ride and the run they can make things a heck of a lot cooler than they really are. Every little bit helps.

Lace-locks

Available at outdoor and camping equipment stores, lace-locks were originally used on sleeping bags and such, but on cycling and running shoes they can save you a lot of time in the transition area: pull the lace up, slip the lock down, and go. Nice.

Bike Computer/Chronometer

There are several makes, some more reliable than others. They can be a big training help, especially for the beginner, because they graphically display your pedaling RPMs—a critical factor in learning consistent spinning technique. Even some top pro triathletes swear by them. The thing to watch out for is letting the

Spiffy, huh? Never underdress on the bike. Wear plenty of warm clothing, well-layered, so you can take it off a little at a time as the day warms up.

computer use you. If you're having a bad day and the stupid thing keeps reminding you of the fact, you've got to be able to turn it off.

Fanny Pack

They're very handy on the bike, especially on long rides, when you're carrying food and you need a place to store a shirt or a pair of tights as the day warms up.

Watch

Your runners'/triathletes' wrist chronometer is an indispensable tool. Buy one that does it all: multiple splits, alarm, countdown mode, etc. Stay away from the kind that beeps a steady cadence—it drives everyone within a 10-mile radius of you crazy.

TRAVELING WITH YOUR GEAR

Traveling to triathlons by air can be an exhausting endurance event in itself. The key is to take every precaution possible, then sit back and let the man fly the plane. Worrying about your $2,000 bike lying broken and bleeding in the cargo hold isn't going to help; it's only going to make your race a little tougher.

Latch on to a good travel agent and plan your trips carefully. If it's possible (and it usually is), meet personally with your agent and explain your special needs. He or she will keep important consideratons on file: you travel with a bike; you need special airline meals; you need to stay in a hotel that will allow you to keep your bike in your room; etc.

The first consideration is buying a bike travel case. I travel a lot—every weekend for stretches during the summertime—so a good case is indispensable. On the other hand, many triathletes who travel only once or twice a season feel they can get by with the kind of simple cardboard box supplied by the airlines. I'd advise against that. Invest in a good case—it's only a matter of time before your unprotected bike is going to show up at the airport on the day before a race you've been working toward for months looking like it's been run over by a truck. Even if you can afford to have a bent frame straightened or a wheel rebuilt, where in the world are you going to have all that done—at any price—at six o'clock on a Saturday night in a strange city?

Both soft and hard bike cases are available. The soft ones are nice in that you don't have to break your bike down. The hard ones are probably somewhat safer. By all means, you should become technically familiar enough with your bike so that you'll be able to put it back together unaided. This can be an intimidating process the first couple of times, so rehearse the procedure repeatedly at home.

After your bike, the most important thing you can bring along is a comprehensive checklist of equipment, tools, and supplies. Compile it well in advance because you'll add items as you go. After you've been to several races and have made all the mistakes you think you can make, consider having the list retyped, then laminated for permanent use.

Traveling to races can be a lot of fun. It can also be a tremendous headache if you haven't prepared properly. Here are a few tips that should help:

1. Travel with the understanding that things are going to go wrong so that you won't get all uptight when they do. Save your jitters for race morning.

2. Use the fact that you're a traveling triathlete to your advantage. Ticket agents, hotel clerks, and other people who can really help you out are often fascinated by the fact that you're "one of those crazy triathletes."

3. Most airlines carry maximums on insurance for checked baggage. You can assure yourself of added coverage by paying for your tickets with an American Express card. Also use a charge card when you book your hotel so that your room will be guaranteed no matter when you arrive.

4. Avoid flights with plane changes. The less your bike gets thrown around, the better.

5. Take plenty of extras: extra tire glue, spare tires, chain lubricant, swim goggles, etc.

6. Choose your hotel carefully. It should be close to the race site *and* have a swimmable pool.

7. Ask for a hotel room on the quiet side of the building (away from the hotel's disco, for instance) and on as low a floor as possible. In hotels where a lot of triathletes are staying, the elevators are always jammed.

8. Take a wet suit and some warm clothes even if the race is being held in Florida in August.

9. If you travel frequently, or to the same events year after year, strike up a trade agreement with a triathlete who races where you live. Offer him or her a place to stay in return for a spot for yourself. That can save you a lot on hotel bills.

10. When traveling to a resort area where you have a choice between staying in a time-share condominium and staying in a hotel, choose the condo. Condos usually have cooking and washing facilities, which makes them cheaper and allows you to eat what and when you want.

11. Many hotels do not allow bikes in the rooms. Check before you make a reservation.

12. There are travel clubs available (USA Amateur is probably the best) that offer rental car discounts, free airfare for your bike on certain airlines, and special hotel and airfare rates. Join one. They can save you plenty.

13. Leave yourself plenty of time at the airport to check in your bike. The tighter your schedule, the less likely you are to arrive at the same time your bike does.

14. Shop the various airline rates for bike transport before you buy a ticket, then bring extra cash. I've seen different ticket agents on the same airline quote different rates for the same flight to athletes standing shoulder-to-shoulder in different check-in lines.

15. If you're traveling with a spouse or friend who likes to follow your race, consider renting a moped for easy course access. On most triathlon courses, private vehicular traffic is strictly controlled.

"I take a nap almost every day. I couldn't do without my nap."—Scott Molina

10
BODY MAINTENANCE: KEEPING THE MACHINE RUNNING SMOOTHLY

You would think that triathletes—the "super-fit, super jocks of the 1980s"—would make their physical well-being the absolute top priority in their lives. It isn't always so.

The line between disciplining yourself to train regularly and being self-compelled to train at all costs is very thin. The line between training hard and training too hard is even thinner. Very often the challenge for the triathlete is not going above and beyond, it's staying within reasonable limits. We push our bodies to perform in competition under terrible conditions and feel a sense of achievement in having done so. Isn't it logical that we should push our bodies to the edge on a daily basis?

No. The endurance athlete who sees his or her body as a mere tool to conquer a physical challenge is on the wrong track. The real challenge *is* your body, not the things it can do. If you're a serious competitive triathlete, the goal is maximum performance through rapid recovery. If you're a participant merely for the joy of it, the goal is total fitness. In both cases the means of achieving the goal is careful, constant maintenance of the human machine.

Eating and drinking enough during an ultratriathlon is critical.

PREVENTIVE MAINTENANCE—TRAINING

Nutrition. You may have noticed that I've studiously avoided talk about nutrition in previous chapters. I'll continue to do so. What generally accepted principles there are are common knowledge: diets high in fat are bad; diets rich in complex carbohydrates—fruits, vegetables, and whole grains—are good. Beyond that, there is little hard, generally agreed upon information. There are carnivorous triathletes and macrobiotic triathletes. One thing for sure, there are few triathletes who eat as well or as poorly as they would like you to think.

I'll leave the preaching on this subject to others. Eat what works. Listen to your body and ignore the fads. Experiment in training and not the week before your biggest race of the year.

Stretching. Unfortunately, the subject of stretching has been editorialized ad nauseum in the national running and triathlon magazines. The competition is keen as to which publication can pose the best looking female model the most suggestively—she's stretching, of course. A lot of runners and triathletes don't stretch simply out of spite.

In my experience, though, stretching *can* help you avoid injuries and speed your recovery from workouts. Being flexible makes it easier to move from one sport to another. It can help you technically, too, especially in swimming, because good freestyle stroke mechanics require plenty of flexibility in the shoulder area.

The problem for a triathlete is finding the time for a regular stretching program. Where possible, incorporate basic stretches into your daily routine. Get into the habit of stretching gently for five minutes prior to each workout, then stretch for another five afterward. Once the habit is formed, the little chunks of

Stretching improves performance and prevents injuries.

quiet will come in handy. They'll ease you comfortably into, then out of, periods of intense activity and give you time to consider what you've just accomplished or what there still is left to do.

Buy a good stetching guide—there's more to stretching technically than meets the eye. Simply bouncing away on tight muscles as so many athletes do is a sure way to pull something important. By no means stretch vigorously before your first workout of the day. Many triathletes stretch only after a training session and never before. They consider the risk of injury too great.

Massage. An hour-long session with a trained sports massage therapist can do wonders for your ability to recover from a long training weekend or a hard race. Better yet, a regular program of massage—once a week or more—will keep your muscles loose, free of lactic acid, and less apt to cramp or tear under stress.

It's important to remember that you're looking for a therapist trained in *sports massage*. He or she will probably use a combination of Swedish massage and more vigorous techniques such as acupressure and *shiatsu* to deal with trouble spots. And boy, will you feel those trouble spots! Be prepared: your first couple of sessions are likely to be a bit painful. The therapist will have to work through knots in muscle fibers and areas of poor circulation due to minor injuries you might have never been aware of.

For that reason by no means get your first massage the day before an important competition. I learned that lesson the hard way before the Ironman in 1982. A big Hawaiian woman gave me her $25 special and I woke up the next morning feeling as if I'd been run over by a truck.

You'll find that, in time, your body will come to "accept" a massage—you'll learn to relax individual muscle groups while the therapist works. His or her fingers will glide over muscle fibers that they were struggling through only a month before. The positive effects of a good massage program are cumulative and far outweigh the substantial cost—a good therapist will charge anywhere from $25–$40 an hour.

Chiropractic. While it's likely that some contemporary chiropractors work in areas beyond their specific area of expertise (diet, immunology, allergic reactions, etc.), the value of chiropractic to athletes in heavy training is impossible to ignore.

The basic concept makes sense: "A body that is not aligned or integrated biomechanically," says Barbara Stewart, a San Diego area chiropractor who has treated several top professional triathletes, "not only must use more energy to function in the same fashion as an aligned body, but the opportunity for a deblitating overuse injury is much higher."

If imbalances exist (and few of us are "ideal" in that sense), training and racing cuts the margin for error. A slight spinal irregularity that might give the average person a sore back on alternate Wednesdays could mean a severe muscle spasm to a triathlete who is pounding away day after day.

The chiropractor's perspective of problem *solving* instead of problem *hiding* is important to a triathlete. Rather than treat symptoms with a bag of ice here and a bandage there, chiropractors look for the cause of the complaint in order to prevent its recurrence. With consistency of training a cornerstone of your triathlon program, staying unhampered by chronic injuries is critical.

A chiropractor with a sports application background might be a good person to consult about a nagging problem you can't seem to shake—an easily adjusted structural imbalance might be at the root of the discomfort, and if you can afford it, regular visits to a chiropractor who knows your body, can keep you in top form. Many top triathletes are convinced of the benefits.

"My training routine doesn't change much week to week and month to month," said Scott Molina after winning the World's Toughest Triathlon in 1984. "I sleep 8–9 hours every night. I get a massage or two every week and I see a chiropractor now almost twice a week."

Orthopedists and podiatrists. It's a good idea for any serious athlete to know where to find help if it's needed. Sports medicine centers, with on-call specialists in several fields, are becoming popular, and you should be aware of the location of one near where you live. Lacking that, know what specialists in appropriate fields near your home have a background or at least an interest in sports medicine. The last thing you want to hear from a doctor who has just looked at your sore knee is, "There's nothing I can do. Don't run." Experienced, concerned orthopedists and podiatrists will keep you on the road, if possible, and can even prescribe alternative forms of exercise as therapy.

Weight Training. As a supplement to triathlon training, weight training, scientifically applied, can probably be of tremendous value to a triathlete. Top athletes in all three individual sports use weights—swimmers and track cyclists most of all—although their use decreases, it seems, as the distances get longer. The enormous thighs of a track cyclist are a testimony to squat-lifting for power; the wiry legs of the endurance cyclist are witness to hundreds of miles of training where the long races are won or lost: on the roads themselves.

As our sport becomes more sophisticated and branches into formal international competition, and the coaching of triathletes blossoms into a fine art, look for weight training by triathletes to become more popular.

For the average triathlete, weight training is likely to be most valuable in two areas:

1. General fitness and appearance—Let's face it, one of the benefits to working out all the time is looking good. Granted, it's what's inside that counts, but carrying the right stuff around in a nice, neat package can't hurt. A general weight and calisthenic program can put the finishing touches on your training by helping you feel tight and well-toned.
2. Pre-season strengthening—With your first race of the year six months away, using supplemental weight training to build weak areas is very effective. If you're a runner with little swimming experience, developing your upper body with weights can be a big help. Or if you have trouble on the bike when it's time to get out of the seat and climb, a month or two of squats can make all the difference in the world.

Where, when, and how to train with weights are big questions for the triathlete pressed for time. In the "how" department, I would recommend you look for a good book on the subject that discusses specific muscles and lifting techniques, because slight variations in how you lift can mean a big difference in the training effect.

Generally, you want to work with light weights and multiple repetitions—use nothing heavier than you can lift 20–25 times in succession. Start with a set of 20 of one particular exercise, then add sets rather than weight as you get stronger. Remember, an endurance athlete isn't looking for bulk. Speed and strength are the goals.

The "when" part depends on the rest of your training program. Weight training will fatigue your muscles more directly than running, cycling, or swimming will, so you should never plan a hard run, for instance, on the day after winning a bet with a friend that you could do ten squat repetitions of a weight he couldn't even get off the ground. The best system is to have a routine that you do regularly—no more than three times a week or so. During the competitive season cut it down to one or two, and concentrate on the upper body—your legs get thrashed enough with all the running and cycling.

Now for the "where." The public choices seem to be limited to one of two extremes: the fitness clubs with the chrome weights, mirrored walls, long lines at each piece of high-tech equipment as if you were waiting for a ski-lift, and plenty of "co-ed opportunities"; or the dank, dark hole-in-the-wall gym where no one weighs less than 200 pounds and eats anything but raw hamburger marinated in protein extract.

The alternative is a home system of your own. You'll probably find like I did that your weight training routine revolves around only a few basic exercises. If it does, try the Scott Tinley "Jed Clampett Weight System." I threw together an odd collection of blocks and pulleys from old sailboats and bricks, flea-market weights, and a water ski handle that works like a charm. It does only what I need it to do, I can use it any time I want, it cost me next to nothing, and it sits right in my own garage, smack in front of a phone and an old black and white TV.

CRISIS MANAGEMENT—RACING

Apart from the specific cautions I've already discussed in previous chapters (pre-race meals and pre-hydration as part of your racing strategy, helmets and clothing on the bike, dealing with cold water on the swim, etc.), your primary personal maintenance concern during a race is fueling and hydrating your body correctly. The only way to learn how to do this is to practice and race—to learn how your body reacts under race conditions and how to respond to problems *before* they occur. If you wait until you need food—and, even more critically, water—then it's too late.

Hydration. If you've ever used a wind-load simulator (an indoor bicycle trainer), you learned very quickly to put an old towel beneath your bike to soak up all the sweat. It saves a lot of wear and tear on both the trainer itself (which rusts) and the carpet (which smells).

You don't perspire any less on the bike when you're outdoors—it's just easy to

miss because the wind blowing in your face is evaporating all the moisture. During the cycling portion of a triathlon you must recognize the fact that you're working hard and sweating—that you need a drink even though it doesn't look or feel like you need to, because if you go into the run already dehydrated, your chances of performing well are slim.

"One thing was going through my head when I started slowing down," said Mark Allen about his collapse at the '84 Ironman, "when I knew the race was over for me as a competitor: 'I've got the training and I've got the ability, but I'm just not smart enough to drink enough.' I guess that's part of the game—it's not just the training, it's knowing what to do during a race."

For short races (triathlons two or three hours in length), your body probably doesn't need anything but water. You may personally prefer something that *tastes*, but it's unlikely that your performance will be improved through use of one of the many electrolyte replacement beverages currently on the market. In some cases, drinking beverages with high concentrations of salts and sugars can actually increase the chances of becoming dehydrated. A highly concentrated solution will tend to hold the water in your belly instead of releasing it into the tissues where it's needed.

In longer races, certain studies have indicated the value of liquid carbohydrate (glucose or other carbohydrate solutions) and electrolyte replenishment. The tremendous variety in commercially available "activity drink" formulas, however, offers evidence that few experts agree on either ingredients or ideal concentrations. Complicating the issue further is the fact that in a race you're at the mercy of whatever product is made available by race officials.

Here's the best solution (the pun was unintentional): experiment in training with a drink that suits you. Don't let your body slide into a condition of chronic dehydration by worrying about drinking enough only during races. Prehydrate sufficiently before the race, then fill both of your water bottles (a triathlete should *definitely* have two water bottle cages on his or her bike) with water and the other with the drink you've become accustomed to in training. After those two bottles are empty, depend primarily on taking water at the aid stations. That will pretty effectively dilute whatever else is available and lessen the chances that you'll react badly to it. Keep in mind at all times that whatever you put down you're going to have to deal with on the run, too. If there are any doubts in your mind, stick to the water, but by all means drink a lot and start drinking sooner than you think you need to.

On the run I would stick mainly to water unless you've had training experience with whatever supplemental drink is being offered. Intestinal cramping and discomfort is often the price of race-day experimentation.

Eating. Once again, your personal experience in training should be the guide in regard to eating. Dave Scott pioneered the use of figs as the ideal Ironman-distance food, but there are triathletes who simply can't eat during competition— to whom food of any kind tastes like cardboard and feels like a mouthful of *papier-mâché.*

As with drinking, you are unlikely to need food in a short or middle distance race. Consider eating only in triathlons of four hours or more in length.

It's important that you eat as early as possible on the bike ride, so that your stomach gets a chance to settle down. Begin as soon as you've caught your breath and have settled into a good pedaling cadence. Bananas are a good choice— they're high in potassium, which can keep you from cramping—as is any soft, sweet fruit like figs or apricots. What you don't want is anything dry. A lot of first-timers at Ironman carry things like granola cookies in fanny packs, then ignore them completely after chewing on the first bite for seven miles and being unable to swallow even *that.*

If your training experience indicates that you "bonk" easily on the bike, by all means bring some food along when you race (use a fanny pack or wear a cycling jersey with pockets in the back). Concentrate first, though, on drinking, and don't fall off your bike trying to peel a banana. Believe me, that's been done more than once.

Dealing with the heat. Heat is the triathlete's worst enemy. I remember sitting with my good friend Ron Smith, one of the best masters triathletes in the world, at breakfast two days before the 1984 Ironman in Hawaii and talking about that. Ron was well into his second enormous plate of eggs, sausages, pancakes, and biscuits for the buffet table at the Kona Surf Hotel. "You know, Scott," he said in-between mouthfuls, "if I didn't know better, and if someone were to suggest that I start a marathon at one o'clock in the afternoon in Hawaii, I'd tell him he was crazy!"

We did it anyway, of course, along with about a thousand other fools. It was a tough day for several reasons, not the least of which was the fact that October 6, 1984, was a record-breaking day in the Islands for heat—98 degrees with humidity in the 80s. No one, not even Dave Scott, races well at Ironman under those conditions. On that day he just survived it better than the rest of us did.

Heat limits your performance perhaps as no other environmental factor can, yet dealing with heat is the triathlete's special talent (or greatest failing).

Triathlon is a warm weather sport, and the run is usually last—in late morning or early afternoon—by which time the sun has worked itself into a frenzy.

How do you deal with heat?

Sometimes there's no way to deal with it other than simply slowing down. The story of marathoner Alberto Salazar's brush with death from heat stroke at the Falmouth Road Race has been told and retold. The race was only seven miles long (7.2, to be exact), but the air was hot and humid, and Salazar was running hard. He collapsed, and his condition was so extreme that he was administered the Last Rites of the Catholic Church.

It's not likely that Salazar became critically dehydrated during a race that short. Rather, the heat, combined with the humidity, conspired against his body's normal heat reduction strategy: increased internal temperature due to exercise will be lowered by sweat evaporating on the skin's surface. In the hot weather, Salazar's intense effort against a world-class field raised his body temperature quickly and he perspired, but in the humidity, the sweat would not evaporate, so a critical link in the defense was lost. So, almost, was Alberto.

Some athletes deal better with heat than others, but all must learn to set a racing pace that will get them to the finish line. Respect the heat. Start slowly in hot weather and find your level gradually. Use water liberally outside as well as inside. Keep your head and face wet: one of the most welcome bits of race course aid I've ever experienced is a baseball cap full of ice. Once the ice melts, though, get rid of the hat. It'll only hold in the heat.

"I've seen pictures of people wearing a hat in the Ironman," Doctor Mac Larsen of San Diego says, "and I ask myself 'What are they *doing*?' The intention I guess is to keep the sun off their heads, but with the head accounting for about 10 percent of the body's heat loss, a hat is only making things tougher. I'd recommend a visor if you have to wear something."

On very hot days, you may find wearing a white, cotton mesh singlet to be cooler than bare skin. The cloth will hold a certain amount of water that will keep you cool as it evaporates. The flapping of the shirt will add to the effect, so don't tuck it in. Generally, white or light-colored clothing is best when the sun is strong.

Remember on hot days that the faster you go, the faster the core temperature of your body will rise (a la Alberto). Give yourself a little margin for error and be aware of the warning signs: if your skin is goose-fleshy and you feel cold even on a hot day; if you're disoriented and nauseous; if you have a headache or you're dizzy and light-headed—then you're showing signs of heat injury. You can stop and walk it in. You can flag a ride to the medical tent. Or you can push yourself to the wall and spend the night in the hospital, although I'll guarantee there's not a hospital in the world that will let you ride your bike through the halls.

"We are immersed in a lifestyle that we like. I'm sure we could pick another career—go out and make lots of money doing something else—but it's a great life."—professional triathlete Dale Basescu, from Encinitas, California

"What's your plan?" Diana Nyad of ABC television interviews leader Jennifer Hinshaw in the run at the Ricoh Ironman in Los Angeles in 1983.

11
A DAY IN THE LIFE

There are no magic answers in this sport, although none of us really ever stops looking. I remember when Scott Molina and I wondered together about Mark Allen after he beat us both for the first time in San Diego back in 1982. At the time, Mark was receiving some support from a local vitamin company and was wearing a shirt with its logo on his chest. "It must be the vitamins," Molina and I told each other. "We gotta get some of those vitamins."

How do you become a triathlete? Do a triathlon. How do you become a more successful triathlete? Do more triathlons.

The advice in this book is just that: advice. It's truth only if it helps. What you're getting are guidelines and tips from someone who's been there, but, like I said, there are no magic answers.

People have said to me after clinics: "I can't relate when you talk about six-minute miles," or "I have time for only 100 miles a week on my bike. See, I have this job. . . ."

I feel bad about those questions because they mean I haven't gotten the basic point across: that my suggestions have to fit into their lives. I fully realize that my training program would be insane for anyone with a full-time job.

It's important to keep in mind that I'm not preaching the one true way of triathlons. Any expert that does so is a fool. File the specific mileage and times for future reference, but consider the concepts carefully. I vary my training by using a combination of long runs, interval training, and recovery runs. I think it's a good plan, and I'd recommend you give it a try. If 20 miles a week is all the running you can handle, break the program down proportionately. Triathlon training must fit into a package of your own design. If it doesn't, you're going to be dropping pieces all over the street until eventually you let the whole thing go and simply walk away.

How *do* triathletes fit triathlons into their lives? You could never count the ways, but the profiles that follow will give you a glimpse into the daily routines of seven athletes who have come to terms with training and racing in three sports.

Of the seven, Mike Adamle is the most demographically typical: a successful white-collar professional in his mid-30s. But I've chosen also to feature three men over the age of 50. For the most part, this is because to me, older triathletes ("Masters" is the term used in the sport for competitors over age 40) represent the reality of the total fitness movement. Staying in shape is a snap when you're in your 20s and 30s. The need for a defined commitment increases dramatically after that.

In addition, the three men, presented consecutively, offer a nice cross-section of levels of triathlon involvement, regardless of age. One is a back-of-the-packer who trains and competes without expectation beyond personal achievement. The second is a self-employed professional who is relatively new to the competitive scene and to competitive success. The third is a man to whom competition and upper-level fitness have long been a way of life. I find their individual adaptations to the triathlon lifestyle fascinating.

EMILIO DESOTO, MONTEREY, CALIFORNIA

Born: November 30, 1932
Height: 5'10"
Weight: 145

Emilio could do a triathlon a week for the rest of his life and never challenge himself the way he did by arriving in Miami from Cuba in 1962. In the construction business (his father was an architect) when Fidel Castro's soldiers took over the island in 1961, Emilio spent six months applying for postrevolution permission to leave the country. Finally, it came through, but Emilio, along with his wife and two sons, left everything they owned behind: their home, their money, their belongings. "We arrived in Miami flat broke," Emilio says in a voice that reflects his native language, "but thanks to God and the Church, we made it. For us, the United States was the land of opportunity."

He worked in Miami for several years at a variety of jobs, then came to California during the late '60s and got back into the construction business, then took a position with the Navy in Monterey. He's still there today, as a construction supervisor at the Naval Postgraduate School.

Emilio became involved in triathlons in 1983 when his son, Emilio, Jr., already competing in the sport, came home with a new bike and gave the old one to Dad.

"I used to swim a little bit just for the fun of it," Emilio, Sr., says, "and run a little bit. My son said to me, 'Dad, now that you're doing all three sports, you should start doing triathlons.' I told him I'd try."

Emilio's first race was on Father's Day in June 1983 at the Foster City Triathlon in northern California, some four months after he had begun to train.

"It was a 4-mile run, a 10-mile bike, and a 1-mile swim," Emilio remembers. "The swim was last, and when I looked at the course I said, 'Holy mackerel!' It looked so long! When I finished, I was real happy."

He was also hooked. He competes now several times a year, although his primary—perhaps only—motivation is to "have fun."

Tuesday is a typical weekday for Emilio DeSoto. He rises at six, eats a bowl of cornflakes, drinks a cup of coffee and a glass of juice, then pedals off to work on his bike. "It's only 3 miles from my house to the job," he says, "but I take the scenic route—14 miles."

Emilio's daily ride takes him along the spectacular coastline of the Monterey Peninsula, through the town of Monterey itself, then onto the naval base. The ride lasts about an hour.

He works until noon, then goes for a four-mile run during lunch. With a stretch before and after and a shower, he's gone for about an hour. "After that, I have a sandwich at my desk while I'm doing my paperwork. The rest of the afternoon I'm in the field at the job site, climbing up and down stairs. That's good exercise, too."

At 4:30 Emilio cycles home—the short route this time, although two of the three miles are uphill without any breaks. "It's a good climb," he says. Once home, he grabs a piece of toast and a glass of juice, then drives off to the Pacific Grove High School for a swim at 5:30.

"The swimming really relaxes me after a day at work," he says. "I swim a mile freestyle and half a mile with paddles and pull buoys."

By seven he's back in the house, where his wife, Maria Theresa, usually has a big bowl of spaghetti waiting for him. It's his favorite meal, and he enjoys it at least three times a week along with a salad and glass of milk.

"My wife takes care of me in that part," Emilio says proudly. "She backs me up 100 percent. She's with me at all of my races."

His weekday schedule pretty much holds true Monday through Thursday. Friday is an easy day on which he'll do only one or at most two of the three sports. One of the weekend days he'll take off completely, with the other being devoted to either a long run or a long ride. "When I was training for the San Francisco Marathon in 1985," he says, "I was running as far as 15 to 18 miles. Usually it's only 9 or 10. My long bike ride is 20 to 25 miles."

Altogether, Emilio DeSoto spends 20 to 30 hours a week training for triathlons. That allows him to finish races like the Bud Light USTS events (1.5K swim, 40K bike, 10K run) comfortably in slightly more than 3 hours.

"I hope someday I can go to Hawaii to do the Ironman," Emilio says. "It's a dream. I want to do the Ironman as a father/son team, but I think that it will be in a few years. Until then, as long as I'm enjoying the sport I'll keep doing it. It's like I say to my wife when I start out in a race on my bike: 'See you when I finish. Don't expect a miracle!' "

DONALD OAKLEY, SEATTLE, WASHINGTON

Born: September 29, 1925
Height: 5'10"
Weight: 155

Donald Oakley is a typical triathlete in one very basic sense: he isn't typical. Born in New Haven, Connecticut, he grew up to be an American Baptist minister, a Navy chaplain, and finally, a practicing clinical psychologist. He also grew up to become a marathoner and later a triathlete. As he himself admits, his greatest challenge and greatest success has been integrating his social life, his professional life, and his sporting life into a single package that works.

In 1969, after a 15-month stretch as a Navy chaplain in Antarctica, Don was transferred to the Navy Regional Medical Center in San Diego, where he underwent clinical sensitivity training preparation for his new duties. It was a combination of that training—of seeing new solutions to problems he had never faced before—and having to deal with important personal problems of his own that changed his life.

"It was a whole new world," he says. "I began looking for graduate programs in clinical psychology in the area and studying in my off-duty time."

Don obtained his Ph.D. in clinical psychology from U.S. International University in San Diego in 1971. The Navy promptly sent him to counsel American soldiers and their families in Taipei, Taiwan, and later to Whidbey Island, Washington, where he eventually retired after 20 years of service in 1979.

In good shape all his life, Don took up running in 1977 and completed his first marathon, the Portland Marathon, a year later in 3:40. Thereafter he trained regularly and completed four more marathons until an Achilles tendon problem cropped up just before his sixth in 1982 and took him off the road. It was while looking for a later race in a national running magazine that he found an alternative: six weeks away was the first U.S. Triathlon Series event on Mercer Island, Washington. "I never knew such a thing existed!" Don remembers.

But he couldn't resist. Despite not having much of a cycling background ("I hadn't been on a bike in 38 years!" he says with a laugh), Don rested his sore tendon by swimming and cycling, then did the triathlon and got through it without a hitch. He was hooked.

"The toughest part for me was the rough-water swim," he says. "I was concerned about hypothermia. Just coming out of the water was a great moment for me."

In 1983, Don was back with an expanded triathlon schedule, and by '84 he had become a dedicated and knowledgeable triathlete, with a well-structured training program and a well-defined set of competitive goals. In September of that year, he fulfilled the biggest of them by becoming the Bud Light USTS National Champion in the 55–59 age group. Racing had become an important part of his life. "I didn't expect to win the championship," he says. "I was like a kid at Christmas."

Things got tougher, though, in 1985, when Don bought his partner's portion of the joint psychology practice. His carefully structured training schedule was shattered by new professional obligations. He considered giving up triathlons altogether. "I was sure I had to give it up," he says. "In a situation like that, it's a great temptation to think you know what the answer will be."

But he resisted the temptation and trained instead around a new work schedule that kept him in the office from eight to eight on Monday, Wednesday, and Thursday and from one to eight on Tuesday. To his surprise, he not only maintained his previous competitive performance level but improved.

For Don Oakley, the normal weekday begins at 5:15 A.M. He has a cup of Sunrise (a coffee-based drink with chicory), shaves, and goes through a brief stretching routine. He's out the door by 6:00 for a 45- to 60-minute run or bike. Then he showers and dresses and heads for the office. It's four miles away, and there are days when he'll ride in on his bike just to pick up the spare mileage.

On Tuesdays, when he has more time in the morning, Don will take a 3-mile run to the local Nautilus fitness center, where he'll work with the weights for 30 minutes or so. Then he'll run back home, eat some dry cereal, and jump into the car for the 20-minute drive to the pool. Tuesday's swim is usually 3,000 yards long, with a 1,200-yard warm-up and 1,800 yards worth of intervals. He swims alone, without a coach, but he remembers the formal instruction he received in late 1983 as a big help.

"It was like learning to swim again," he says. "What I thought was a good stroke was really *lousy*! My swim stage is now my best."

With Friday, Saturday, and Sunday off, every weekend is a long one for Don Oakley. That situation would be a luxury for most working people, but it presents a problem to Don because, while he needs the mileage, he must be careful not to pack too much into too short a time. He repeats his short runs to the Nautilus center and back on Friday and puts in a long swim later in the day— 4,500 yards, with a 1,200-yard warm-up and a long-distance (1,000 yards or more) time trial.

On Saturday, Don Oakley does what he calls a "training triathlon," which is exactly what it sounds like. "The only difference between that and a regular triathlon," he says, "is that the breaks are longer and I do the events at sub-race speed."

Sunday for Don is a single-sport day. He takes a long bike ride of between 30 and 50 miles over varied terrain and usually doesn't run, so he's set up nicely for the work and training week ahead.

"In the last 10 years," he says, "I've focused on the principle that, when things get in the way of what you do, just fly with it and do what you can. I've been amazed at the success of that policy.

"I suspect I'll be doing triathlons until I can't do them."

RON SMITH, DEL MAR, CALIFORNIA

Born: July 13, 1933
Height: 6′
Weight: 175

Ron Smith is the ultimate dive-right-in, grit-your-teeth-and-bear-it endurance athlete. A former member of the Navy's Underwater Demolition Team, Smith has been a football player, a weight lifter, a springboard diver, and a surfer, just to name a few. He's also a highly successful businessman and entrepreneur; he founded the popular Chart House Restaurant chain. Now he's a triathlete—the Bud Light USTS National Champion in his age group, with a personal best at the Ironman of 11:52 (at age 50)—and to hear him tell it, he'll be a triathlete for life.

"Oh, I got into it for the challenge like everybody else," says Ron. He's a big, tremendously built, red-faced man whose current lifestyle allows him days at a time without a shave, so he can look particularly gnarled and fierce at times. But he is a humble, sensitive man, generous with his time and his advice. "I guess triathloning isn't different than any other challenge, but I remember the first Ironman in '78, and how everyone thought those 13, 14 people were crazy. I had to have some of that."

Ron has had a *lot* of that. He's a prodigious trainer and competitor. In 1984 alone he logged 25,000 miles on his bicycle. Only injuries—and he's survived some serious, spectacular crashes over the years—can take him off the road. And even at their worst, they never take him off for long.

The scariest of his crashes came during the summer of 1983, when Ron's front tire blew on a steep, fast downhill. Over the bars he went, breaking a number of bones, his left leg worst of all. A major operation—and several pounds of hardware—were required to put everything back together. "Lucky man," they said. "Lucky to live, let alone walk." But Ron was swimming within weeks after the operation and riding a stationary bicycle at home soon after that. Incredibly, four months after the terrible fall, he completed his fourth Ironman in a little over 12 hours, 40 minutes.

"It was kind of a stupid thing to do," admits Ron, who was surrounded by people, including his wife, who were hoping he wouldn't enter the event. "I had a lot of second thoughts before the race. But I'd been putting in a lot of rehabilitation miles on the bike and truly believed that I was under control during the race. I just couldn't stand the thought of not being fit enough to do that."

Seldom in his life has Ron Smith not been fit enough.

An early riser, he gets in most of his training before noon. On a typical day he is moving through a half-hour session of combined weight training and stretching by 5:15. "You know us old guys," he jokes. "We don't need a lot of sleep." After that, he runs six miles or so near his home in Del Mar, California, then jumps in his VW van and drives to the Jewish Community Center pool in La Jolla, where he trains with a Masters swim team. During most of the year he'll average 10,000–15,000 yards a week in the pool, building to 20,000 for his peak competitive season. Ron's weakest link by far in the triathlon is swimming, so he's religious about getting in the water and working hard. Almost all of his yardage is in the form of intervals.

After swimming comes the bike—the machine itself is usually located right where he can find it: in the back of the van. His daily ride is anywhere from 25–50 miles, north or south along the scenic Pacific Coast Highway, and his average weekly miles can total a heart-thumping 500.

The cornerstone of Ron's training is one ultradistance run and one or two ultradistance bike rides per week, month in, month out. Building up to a 20-mile run for a specific event without a consistent base takes too long, he maintains, and it's the same on the bike.. So he'll pedal off on the famous Wednesday morning group ride from Del Mar to Dana Point (80–100 miles), ride long again (60–100 miles) on Saturday, and hit the trail for a 16–20-mile run on Sunday. With those three workouts under his belt he's ready for anything year-round.

In addition to his regular morning mileage during the week, Ron puts in a lot of what he refers to as "junk miles." These are supplemental rides ("not so much running," he says, "and every time I swim I'm anaerobic anyway, so nothing's junk in the pool.") done at low intensity, often for no reason other than pure enjoyment.

"A lot of those bike miles shouldn't even *be* there," he says, "but I get a certain amount of mental well-being out of it. You feel a little superior when you can crank the miles on—it makes me feel better about my overall ability.

"Besides," he laughs, "you can eat more!"

Ron Smith will be the first to tell you that he is totally sold on fitness. But he admits his own excesses, and cautions other triathletes against them. "I try to keep it round," he says. "Family, business, sports. There have been times when it got awful lopsided in the sports area for me. In that sense, with regard to my personal and marital life, the sport has been detrimental.

"There just has to be a time when you say, 'Hey, let's go to the beach, let's go to a movie, let's take a walk.' You can't let it get so intense that you become one-sided."

BETH MITCHELL, WILLIAMSTON, MICHIGAN

Born: January 2, 1964
Height: 5′3″
Weight: 104

Like many top professional triathletes, Beth has a strong swimming background, and while she can't boast the former All-American swimming status of some of her triathlon peers, her experience in the water combined with natural speed and strength in the other two events brought her right to the top from the very start. In 1984, just 20 years old, with little experience and no reputation as a top triathlete, she came from behind to win the 1984 Bud Light U.S. Triathlon Series National Championship. She was suddenly faced with a decision she never thought she'd have to make: Was there a future for her as a professional triathlete?

For 10 years, until she graduated from Okemos High School in East Lansing, Michigan, in 1982, Beth was an age group swimmer. Her specialty was the breaststroke. When the sport of triathlon rolled around, she was ready ("I'd been doing the three sports just for fitness anyway").

"The competition appealed to me," she said. "I'd never gone where I wanted to in swimming. I had more to achieve."

During her first year in the sport, Beth was a student at Michigan State University, so she had to fit what she calls "sporadic" training around classes and an assortment of part-time jobs. She'd get up around six in the morning, stretch, and do calisthenics for a half-hour, then put in a run of 6–8 miles. After that, she would ride the 7 or so miles to school on her bike. She found that a big time-saver was getting all of her classes scheduled in a single block so that once her last class was over she was free either to ride to work or to ride for real, weather permitting, for 20–30 miles. Then, at 5:00 P.M., she'd head back to school to the pool.

With school on hold and a professional triathlon career pending, Beth is freer with her time. A typical day starts at 9:00 A.M., probably with some light stretching and a series of calisthenics. "I'm religious about that kind of stuff," Beth laughs. Then she's out the door with a five- to eight-mile run. Plagued with injuries after her win at the National Championships in '84, she's cautious about running too much and finds that the training in three sports has helped a lot in that respect. "I'm definitely getting by on fewer miles," she says. "That's

important, because I've got to work for consistency. The injuries have really thrown me off."

Twenty minutes after her run—after a change of clothing and something to drink—Beth is off on a 20–30-mile bike ride through the rolling farmland of the East Lansing area. She rides hard, conscious of quality, making the most of her time. She eats when she gets home, spends a few hours working at a local running store, then heads to the pool.

In the summer, Beth swims during open swim at the big University of Michigan 50-meter outdoor facility in East Lansing. She swims on her own and enjoys the solitude after her years as a competitor in that sport, although she admits that to get where she wants in triathlons she may have to get into a more structured program.

She swims between 2,500 and 3,500 meters a day, with a long, straight 1,000–2,000 meters in the beginning; a variety of intervals in the middle; and some short, fast 50s at the end. The final workout of a summer day then follows: 3–4 miles of running through Michigan State campus or 15–20 miles of cycling. After that, it's home for dinner.

"I don't eat red meat or fried foods," says Beth, "but my diet is pretty normal. I eat a lot of ice cream, though. I think I eat more of that than most people."

The cold weather and snow of the Michigan winter make training more of a challenge for Beth, although her routine doesn't stray from the summer regimen very much at all. The running doesn't, definitely. "The winter is no fun," she says. "I don't even like to think about it. But I've been out there in subzero weather and never had any problem. I just dress for it."

Biking of course, is a different story, and for that there's an indoor trainer that Beth, like most cyclists and triathletes, hates. Still, it's necessary so she pedals in front of her television set or with her earphones hooked up to a stereo for a good hour every day.

Young and new to the sport, Beth Mitchell is not about to rush into more of a triathlon than she can handle. "I really think my talent is in the longer distances," she says, "but I haven't done a lot of distance training to this point. I don't want to wear myself down. I've got goals ahead."

MARILYN AVERY, MANHATTAN, KANSAS

Born: March 15, 1945
Height: 5'5½"
Weight: 110

There aren't a lot of triathletes in Kansas. There are even fewer female triathletes there. What this means for Marilyn Avery and her close friend and training partner, Donna Miller, is that "everyday" triathlon equipment like cleated cycling shoes and wool pants for cycling on cold days are unavailable at local shops. They must be special-ordered, then reordered if they don't fit. "There just aren't many cyclists my size," says Marilyn, who spent some time cycling with plastic bags over her feet before the arrival of a new pair of thermal cycling booties. "It's a real drawback," she says, "and *nobody* carries tri-suits."

Ragged supply lines are only one problem among many for triathletes in parts of the country where severe winters and a lack of recognition of the sport go hand in hand. A place to train when the Great Outdoors closes down is another.

"In 1984," says Marilyn, "we had two, three weeks where it got down to 20 below zero. I've tried to run when it's like that but it hurts my knees. The rest of my body stays warm enough, but it just hurts my knees."

So she runs on the fieldhouse track at Kansas State University, near where the Averys live—seven laps to a mile—on days when the temperature is extreme. Through most of the winter, though, she braves the cold and wind in the name of fitness.

Marilyn lives with her husband Bill and their two children Bryant and Mary Ellen, in a big house on College Avenue near the center of town. They bought the house in 1983, then spent two years adding to the original structure. The job was easier than it might have been due to the fact that Marilyn and Bill own a small subcontracting construction firm, but it still took a lot of time and energy. Cramming a triathlon training program into a life already bulging with activity was a challenge in itself.

If anyone was equipped for it, Marilyn was. Naturally competitive, she's always been attracted to the unusual and the inaccessible. She met her husband Bill in Cocoa Beach, Florida, in 1970, where they were both flight instructors. She'd learned to fly two years before on a kind of personal dare. "I was seeing a guy who was in military flight training," she says. "I thought it would be fun to solo before he did." So she did.

Triathlons offered her the same kind of opportunity. The sport was new, different and, says Marilyn, "I fell in love with cycling." Besides, tennis tournaments took too much of her weekend and just running was boring. In her very first race, "The Topeka Tin Man" in 1982, she missed first place in her age group by a whisker. She was hooked.

By 1985, Marilyn was a triathlon veteran and a local hero. That year, she placed an impressive second in her age group at the huge Chicago Bud Light USTS race in August and sixth at the USTS National Championship in late September. Best of all, she never stopped having fun.

Marilyn likes to do as much of her training as early in the day as possible, so during the week, she's on the road well before six, running and cycling on alternate days. Her weekly totals for the two sports average about 20 miles for the run and 100 miles for the bike. She swims between three and four miles a week.

Monday is a long run day: ten miles. Wednesday is a long ride. Weather permitting, she and several friends bike 30 miles through hilly pastures and to the little town of Westmorland. They have lunch there and ride back. The riding itself takes between three-and-a-half to four hours or more depending on the infamous Kansas winds. The entire trip, though, can take much longer than that. "When we eat lunch, it can take a long time," Marilyn laughs.

Except for Wednesday, Marilyn is back in the house after her morning workout by seven, so she can get the kids off to school. She usually swims at noon—on her own, 2,000–2,500 yards—at the Kansas State pool. Afternoons are devoted to keeping the house in shape and to business details. One nice aspect of the Avery's self-employment is an office for Marilyn at home. Bill works at the company office in an industrial park outside of town.

Unlike most triathletes, Marilyn keeps her weekends free. Except for an early morning run here and there, Saturdays and Sundays are "family time." Her priorities seem balanced and well-defined: despite her success in the sport, she is by no means a triathlon fanatic.

"I don't know how long I'll be doing triathlons," she says. "I just know I enjoy the training as much as I've enjoyed anything."

JOHN GARCIA, CORONA DEL MAR, CALIFORNIA

Born: June 27, 1955
Height: 5′9″
Weight: 175

Relatively few triathletes have done the Hawaii Ironman, but most wish they had. While it certainly can be said that ultradistance triathlons are not for everyone, it's hard to ignore the mystique of the Ironman and the role it plays for athletes in this sport.

"I started training for the Ironman to fill a void in my life," says John Garcia, a southern California architect who had been a casual triathlete for more than a year before he was bitten by the Ironman bug. "I'd seen the Julie Moss finish on television in 1982 like everyone else and that inspired me to get involved in the sport in the first place. But then I read a quote by somebody in an article about the race that said 'It's a bunch of ordinary people doing extraordinary things.' That struck me."

Bored with his job and facing the prospect of dealing with a broken personal relationship, John decided in December of 1984 to train for the next Ironman. "It gave me a focus for my energies," he says. "I didn't want to dwell on something negative."

John's career as a triathlete began at the tail end of the 1983 triathlon season. He'd played football (offensive guard) at Los Alamitos High School and some "occasional" racquetball since, but that was the extent of his physical conditioning. In no way was he a highly trained endurance athlete when he entered his very first race, the short-distance Seal Beach Triathlon, in September 1983.

"It was a lot harder than I thought it would be," John remembers. "I thought I'd finish in the top half of the field. Instead I was 520th out of 650."

But John stayed at it, training for races on five or six workouts per week, usually no more than one workout per day. "I think my longest ride was something like 30 miles," he says. "My longest run was five or six. I enjoyed the training, but it was not the top priority in my life. When the Ironman came up that changed."

And how. In January, 1985, John talked to one of the few triathlon coaches in the nation, Mark Evans, of Lafayette, California, and put together a daily program that incorporated a full range of workouts, from speed work to over-distance training to regular maintenance mileage. By May of that year, when John's acceptance into the Ironman by way of the lottery came through, he had a good base established and was ready to put in some long hours.

On most weekdays during his Ironman training John was out of bed before 5:30 A.M. He threw his work clothes into a bag and was in the Newport Beach YMCA pool by six. Swimming alone, he put in between 2,500 and 3,500 yards' worth of assorted intervals. He was in the office by 7:30.

Usually, his second workout of the day didn't happen until after work. Monday was a recovery ride (15 miles) after a tough session on Sunday. On Tuesday he rode hard: hills and intervals, about 35 miles, and Thursday was much the same. Wednesday called for a 4–6 mile run followed by a ten-miler the next morning. On Friday evening, he ran a mixed-pace seven miles, with some fast stuff in the middle.

John's Saturdays and Sundays were typical for a triathlete: a good weekend means two good, long workouts. Saturday was bike day—up before dawn and on the road for 4–6 hours, 80–100 miles, with a short 10-minute run following just to get him used to the bike/run transition. On Sunday he ran between 15 and 18 miles.

In the end, the program worked almost perfectly. John Garcia finished the 1985 Ironman in Hawaii in 13 hours, 24 minutes, and 49 seconds. The last seven miles were tough—his marathon time was five hours and 42 minutes—but the basic goal had been achieved.

"It was worth more than the thirteen-and-a-half hours I spent out there," he says. "It was worth the ten months that I spent training for it, because I learned a lot about myself physically and mentally. I gained a lot of confidence in myself and I shed 25 pounds—something that had been bugging me for 15 years. It really changed me as a person."

It changed him as a triathlete, too. Much of what he learned during the 1985 season will carry over into the shorter races in 1986 and beyond. He found the regular long runs and rides to be especially helpful. "They really brought me up a couple of levels," he says. "And now I know the limits of my body. I can push a lot harder on the bike without worrying about spoiling my run. After the Ironman, I know I'll always be able to finish no matter what."

MIKE ADAMLE, CHICAGO, ILLINOIS

Born: October 4, 1949
Height: 5'9"
Weight: 195

It's not a long way—a couple of blocks, max—from Soldier Field, home of the Chicago Bears football team, to Solidarity Drive, site of the Adler Planetarium, the Shedd Aquarium, and the world-famous Field Museum of Natural History.

For Mike Adamle, though, Soldier Field and Solidarity Drive must have seemed a universe apart. It was 10:00 A.M. on the morning of August 18, 1985. Adamle was a competitive athlete for the first time since he'd hung up his helmet as a Chicago Bears running back in 1977. But this time there was no roar of a huge, partisan crowd echoing back and forth across the floor of a football stadium, no gruff words of encouragement from massive teammates, no hard smack of protective plastic on plastic, or dull thuds and grunts of solid contact. Mike Adamle was a triathlete, or was trying to become one at least. Solidarity Drive and the finish line of the Chicago edition of the Bud Light US Triathlon Series triathlon were still 30 minutes away. None of the fancy moves he'd learned as an All-American at Northwestern University could help him now. The spectators along the way could cheer, but they couldn't block. Mike was on his own, thinking, as all triathletes do at times, that with just a little more training under his belt, he'd be feeling a heck of a lot better.

The 1985 Chicago race—Mike's first as a participant—was not his initial exposure to the sport. I met him in 1982 after I had won the February Hawaii Ironman. Mike was working for NBC television at the time and we were both in New Zealand for the "Survival of the Fittest" contest. He'd seen ABC's coverage of the Ironman and had been impressed. He talked a lot about triathlons.

In late 1983, Mike became a sports reporter and anchorman for WLS-TV in Chicago, a national ABC affiliate. The following August, he got a long, long look

at the 1984 Chicago USTS, acting as the finish line announcer for a race that broke its own record for athlete participation in a single event. It was a tough morning, but Mike stuck it through, doggedly hanging on to the mike until the last finisher had crossed—past the four-hour mark and after the race crew had begun to dismantle the finish line.

"Mike *made* the race for that last finisher," recalled Cathy Moy, public relations director for the US Triathlon Series. "He had a real empathy for the athletes—he was right there with them the whole way."

"There are times in my business," says Mike, "that I feel a little like a parasite—talking about people in sports, but never doing anything myself. After announcing at that race I said to myself, 'Next year, I'm gonna *do* this.' "

There was another factor involved in the decision, too.

"One day I woke up and looked in the mirror and wanted to throw up," says Mike. "I'd let myself go like a lot of people do."

So he started training in March for the 1985 race. He had six months to get in shape. He'd never owned a ten-speed, so he bought a bike and began to ride four days a week. On a typical morning, he was up at 6:30. He'd stretch, eat a light breakfast, and then head south along Lake Shore Drive from his home in Lincoln Park. Three times a week he'd run after the ride—up to seven miles—trying to get his legs ready for the bike/run transition of the triathlon. He was in the studio by 10:00 A.M.

Regular hours, however, are not a luxury most people working in the media often get to enjoy. Mike's were typically erratic. Workouts were often squeezed in-between shows—he once detoured on a bike ride to drop by Wrigley Field and cover the retirement announcement of Chicago Cubs shortstop Larry Bowa.

Still, with the help of one long ride per week of 30 miles, Mike's weekly bike mileage climbed toward 100. His running mileage stayed over 30, but his swimming still needed some help. "Three weeks before the race I couldn't do ten laps of the pool without stopping," Mike laughs.

A crash-coaching program he received at the Court Club in downtown Chicago helped. A week before the race he swam a mile in Lake Michigan— where the triathlon swim would be held—without any problem. He was ready. Someone else was going to have to do the announcing.

Someone did. And not even a pair of young, angry linebackers could have kept Mike Adamle, triathlete, from the finish line. His time: three hours, two minutes, and 46 seconds.

"All I could think about as I crossed the finish line was 'I did it, man!' " says Mike. "I couldn't stop talking. It was a real adrenaline high—the kind of thing you can't bottle and sell in a pharmacy."

Then he went on to compare two very different sports: "The triathlon is not so much like a football game itself. It's parallel to training camp when you have two-a-day sessions with the temperature up around 95. There are times there when you wanted to get on your hands and knees and say you can't do it anymore."

But Mike never stopped as a football player and he wasn't about to stop as a triathlete. "If my shoelace would've come untied during the race," he laughed, "I wouldn't have stopped to tie it!"

A YEAR IN MY LIFE

Lastly, there's me: Scott Tinley. Six feet tall, one hundred fifty-five pounds. I was born on October 25, 1956 and my birthday in 1985 fell just one day before the Ironman. Winning that race for the second time and breaking Dave Scott's record were a heck of a way to celebrate.

What does it take to be a top triathlete? There's a certain amount of natural talent, of course, but what it takes more than anything is long hours of hard work.

Our bodies are incredible machines, capable of going and going and going, assuming that we give them time to adjust to increasing demands. I've found over the years, as I've mentioned elsewhere in this book, that consistency of training is terribly important.

The key to predictable, steady performance is a year-round program that varies in intensity with the seasons, but varies little in quantity. At least that's what has worked for me, and it's what works for Scott Molina, and I think it's fair to say that the two of us race much more frequently and with much more success than anyone else in the business.

Here's the way my year went in 1985, leading up to the Ironman victory. Without a doubt it was the most successful season of my career, so I must have been doing something right.

December/January. My mileage was down perhaps 20% over the peak periods of 1984. I was concentrating primarily on recovering from the season—the ultradistance races I'd done in the Fall (Nice and Ironman) and the late, but reasonably long professional race in Kauai in December.

To facilitate mental recovery, I let myself drift a bit away from the triathlon. I caught up on long-neglected social obligations, did some yard work and personal projects. Skiing took me away from training, and so did surfing and tennis.

When I did train, speedwork and hard workout days were a low priority.

Maintenance mileage was the goal. I was putting in 17,000 yards a week in the pool, 350 miles a week on the bike, and 60 miles a week running.

I understand that's more mileage than most triathletes will ever log during even their biggest week. Keep in mind, though, that it took me years to get to the point where my body could handle it. And that my profession—my *job*—is being a triathlete. A good one.

February/March. The mileage began to pick back up and the training emphasis was on endurance, strength, and fast recovery from workouts. On the bike I rode frequently in high gears, so the pedals were tough to push all the time, and I concentrated on not coasting down hills unless it was absolutely necessary. I looked for courses with plenty of hills every time I went out running or cycling. That made the legs strong, and several workouts a week with the weights did the same for my upper body. When the weather was bad—weather that I might have used as an excuse *not* to train in January—I hopped on the wind trainer and kept an eye on technique. The winter months are a great time to iron out technical flaws in any of the three sports.

During this period I was also very conscious of preventive maintenance: I was religious about stretching, using the weights for strength, and getting a good massage at least once a week.

April/May. It was time to get organized. The racing season had arrived. Short-distance events, which would continue to be an integral part of my training for the next five months, required only a mild, one-day taper and very little, if any, recovery time. For the professional triathlete this is critical. If you race frequently (and you must to make a living), ordinarily you need to back off from training two days before an event, then recover for a day or two afterward, which means you end up training hardly at all. That leaves you in a tough spot late in the season when it's time for the long- and ultradistance events.

Workouts during this time tend to focus on quality and the mileage is at a season high: 25,000 yards a week in the pool, 425 miles a week on the bike, 75–80 miles a week running.

June/July/August. I was racing almost every weekend—mostly short-distance events that took around two hours to complete. Naturally, I was travelling frequently, too, moving from coast to coast and stopping sometimes in the middle for events like the Champion Auto Triathlon in Minnesota, the Columbus (Ohio) Bud Light Trithlon, and the huge Chicago Bud Light USTS.

During the peak of the season, keeping the mileage up requires plenty of creativity. It inevitably drops off some, but the shortfall is compensated for by the increase in quality. Often, a short race on a weekend morning is only the first part of the training day—a middle distance bike ride (40–50 miles) later on helps keep the legs loose and the endurance capacity high.

With my mind on the long races to come, I was careful during this period to keep up the one over-distance workout a week in each sport: the 20-mile run, the 100-plus-mile bike ride, the two to three-mile ocean swim.

September/October. I was concentrating on the big, important races. I felt very good, and that was certainly the result of the training I had done during the winter when the temptation was to lay back and do nothing. My mileage dropped in mid-September: 19,000 yards swimming, 380 miles a week cycling, 65 miles a week running, although getting in a good workout each time was important. That doesn't mean they were all hard, but it does mean they all fit together; the hard ones leading into the easy ones, the easy ones back into the hard ones. With Nice and Ironman on my mind, it seemed as if every training day was critical. I was careful, too, to get a nap when I felt like one and to maximize any little time I had to rest.

In late September I had a poor race at the Bud Light USTS National Championships on Hilton Head Island and placed fourth. It was the first time all year I'd been out of the top three, and I wasn't pleased, although my mental attitude was still good. The Nice Triathlon was just two weeks away.

I tapered my workouts off a full four days for Nice and felt very fresh and well prepared. On race day (October 13) the swim went well, and I was strong on the big climb into the mountains during the first half of the bike ride. I passed Mark Allen, who had won the race the previous three years, and passed Dave Scott, too. Scott Molina, who I felt I could outrun over 20 miles, was not too far ahead. Then I fell hard on a sharp turn full of loose gravel on the way down, then fell again on the opposite side not 100 yards farther down! Both crashes were bad, but neither put me out of commission. I made it to the bottom, barely in one piece, and finished the bike, then ran well enough to grab second place behind Mark. I flew home very stiff and very sore, with a bunch of "what-ifs" in my head. A win at Nice would have been the high point of the season.

There was hardly time for regrets. Ironman was 14 days away and I could barely walk, let alone train. I tried massage, ultra-sound, electo-acuscope, acupuncture, light cycling, and slow swimming. Still, it was more than a week before I could run. All in all, I got in three good days of training, then a three-day taper before I was treading water in Kailua Bay waiting for the gun. Eight hours, fifty minutes, and 54 seconds later the season, for the most part, was over. For the first time since February, 1982, I was the Ironman champ.

Here's a typical "Day in the Life" of my life. As I said, the mileage can vary, but the basic routine hardly ever does:

      6:30 A.M.: rise, light breakfast, business calls back east
 7:15–8:30 A.M.: run
 8:30–9:00 A.M.: more breakfast
 9:00–12:00 P.M.: ride, end up at the pool
12:00–1:30 P.M.: swim
 1:45–3:30 P.M.: more bike, end up at home
 3:30–4:00 P.M.: lunch, return phone calls
 4:00–5:30 P.M.: work on my "ST" apparel business
 5:30–6:30 P.M.: short run, weight workout or easy ocean swim
                   during the summer
 6:30–7:30 P.M.: jacuzzi, stretch, have a beer
 7:30–8:00 P.M.: dinner
 8:00–10:00 P.M.: relax, spend time with my wife, Virginia
    10:00 P.M.: bedtime

"Boy, it must be hard to be out there for 11½ hours!"—Dave Scott after winning the 1984 Ironman Triathlon in eight hours and 54 minutes

12
MILESTONES—
RACES THAT
MADE A
DIFFERENCE

In the short history of the sport of triathlon, there are milestone races that either highlighted outstanding individual performances or marked the beginning of important trends. Tom Warren's Ironman victory in 1979—and, more importantly, Barry McDermott's reportage of it in *Sports Illustrated*—opened the triathlon door to mass participation. Julie Moss's dramatic Ironman finish three years later knocked down the entire wall, not only bringing huge numbers of athletes into the sport, but opening the eyes and ears of the general public as well.

Those two races have certainly been well-reported and rereported. Others, of only slightly less importance, aren't known far beyond the immediate triathlon community, although their impact, in a dramatic or historic sense, was significant.

The races I've chosen to highlight are merely ones that stand out in my own mind. This isn't a ranking—certain of my peers surely would include some of these races and leave out others. No matter. Better that part of the story be left for someone else to tell—it gives you something to look forward to.

The year 1982 saw a big jump in the popularity and sophistication of the sport. In the wake of the Moss/McCartney Ironman duel came thousands of triathlon hopefuls and plenty of race directors eager to give all of them an arena. There were stirrings within the major media and sports promotion firms, too. ABC television was reaping big benefits from its Ironman coverage. The market looked ripe. The year saw several events that reflected major areas of triathlon growth.

THE UNITED STATES TRIATHLON SERIES
SAN DIEGO

Swim 2K/Bike 30K/Run 15K
June 12, 1982

The inaugural United States Triathlon Series event took place at Torrey Pines State Beach, just north of La Jolla, California. It was a glamorous location, but the conditions were far from ideal. The late spring sky over southern California was heavy and gray, the air was chilly, and the water was a frigid 64 degrees. Still, 600 triathletes showed up to break in an entirely new concept: triathlons for the masses, set into a framework of identical distances in successive cities.

As it turned out, the concept was an attractive one, and the U.S. Triathlon Series grew from a wobbly collection of five West Coast races into a slickly produced road show of international significance. At that first race, however, no one quite knew what to expect—not the producers of the event, Jim Curl and

Carl Thomas, or the athletes. There were rough spots, but they were easily overlooked. Everyone concerned was treading in unexplored waters.

Certainly no one could have expected that the four men who would dominate the sport for so long—through 1982 and beyond—would race head to head for the first time at the San Diego USTS. What gave Dave Scott, Scott Molina, Mark Allen, and me a competitive edge on that day, then continued to give us an edge in hundreds of collective races after that? None of us has been able to come up with an answer. Was it talent? Unlikely. Many athletes with more natural talent than any of us have, marched into, then out of, triathlons without rising to the top. Was it some strange quirk of physiology that gave us special multisport capabilities? Was it simple hard work?

Whatever the reason, by mid-1983, three of us would be training together on a daily basis, Dave Scott would still be Dave Scott, and we would be firmly entrenched within the sport as the "Big Four." In June of 1982, though, we all had a long way to go.

As the defending Ironman champ, I was probably the favorite going into the San Diego race, a position that didn't count for a thing once Dave Scott got rolling. He had a great bike ride over a rough, hilly course and won the race by over four minutes. I was behind him through the entire race—way back in the swim, seventh off the bike, then second on the run for most of the last 6 miles. (The original USTS distances were lightly modified in '83, then changed to the present and final 1.5K/40K/10K distances in 1984.)

Behind me for most of the way was a guy I'd heard about but never met: Scott Molina, from Pittsburg, California. Molina had won some biathlons up north and placed first in the Sierra Nevada Triathlon in 1981, but I had no way of knowing if he was for real or not. Back then, there was always some monster rumored to be able to win by an hour—the fireman from Florida, the rock-climber from Boulder. Molina, though, was a rumor that turned out to be true.

The fourth future member of the club in that San Diego race was Mark Allen, of Del Mar, California, competing in his first triathlon ever. A good swimmer and naturally strong cyclist, he was right with us for a time on the run, until Molina and I dropped him at around 4 miles. Then Molina dropped *me* with 200 yards to go, and I went back to work at the Mission Bay Aquatics Center that afternoon, shaking my head, rightly convinced that it was going to be a long year.

THE HORNY TOAD INVITATIONAL TRIATHLON SAN DIEGO

Swim 1.2 miles/Bike 56 miles/ Run 13.2 miles
August 8, 1982

Two months after the San Diego USTS race, we were back at the same location for the Horny Toad, a small, understated local event that has been blessed over the years with some startlingly good fields. What makes the '82 edition especially

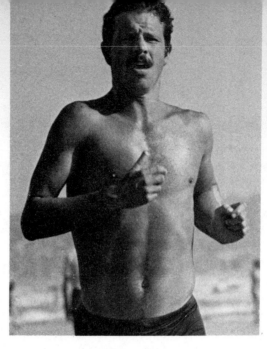

**Rick
Delanty.**

interesting is the fact that it highlighted the tremendous natural ability of Mark Allen and featured a dramatic performance by Julie Leach, of Newport Beach, California. A relative unknown at the time, Leach would win the Ironman two months later, holding off the challenges of several better-known women with the same kind of stubborn determination she displayed in San Diego.

The Horny Toad report that follows comes directly from the *San Diego Running News* (later *Running & Triathlon News*), a local tabloid that was probably the first running publication to treat the sport of triathlon seriously.

For several hundred yards of the long, hot stretch of Sorrento Valley Road, it was just the two of them. No other runner was in sight. Leslie Mendez and Julie Leach were a pair of lonely black silhouettes under the late morning sun. From a distance, they seemed to be barely moving, although you knew that in reality each was putting tremendous effort into every step.

After four and a half hours of competition, it had come to this: Mendez slowly but surely losing the final segments of what had once been a huge lead, Leach working hard to close the remaining gap as quickly as possible, her sharp blue eyes focused not on the road or on the other runner, but on something deep inside herself. Clearly, no distraction was going to intrude upon the will of simple maintenance. "Keep it going," Leach seemed to be saying to herself. "Just keep it going."

For all their logistical complexity, and in spite of all the sophisticated equipment and technology, triathlons have a way of resolving themselves in the most human terms. Most long triathlons end with the run, by which time thoughts of flat tires and sweaty helmets are long forgotten. If you swam an extra 40 yards or got tangled in the kelp, you've forgotten that, too. On the run you're back to basics—two shoes and a pair of shorts like everyone else. On a good day, you're looking to pick up a couple of places. On a bad day, getting to the end of the damn race will suit just fine. At the Horny Toad Triathlon, winners Julie Leach and Mark Allen had very good days indeed.

The morning began the way many coastal southern California mornings do—gray and cool. There was a brief prerace meeting, a quiet walk to the beach, and then an informal start for the 100 invited athletes. There are no frills at the Horny Toad, just tough competition.

First out of the water was Dave Horning, 34, from Berkeley, California. Close behind was 19-year-old Leslie Mendez, sixth overall on the swim and almost 10 minutes ahead of the woman who would come back to haunt her, Julie Leach. Mendez was also 5 minutes ahead of Ironman champ Scott Tinley, who was informed by his wife Virginia during his frantic transition that his chief rival, Scott Molina, was 4 minutes ahead. "*Jeezus*," Tinley hissed in frustration, "what's he doing, wearing *fins*?"

For 20 of the 56 hilly miles of the bicycle route, Horning held the lead. Then Mark Allen, a 24-year-old lifeguard from Del Mar, went by in a rush, and Horning was able to offer only brief encouragement before the newcomer was out of sight. No one, including Allen himself, would have guessed that this was the last time all day that the lead would change hands. In fact, for a while, Allen wasn't even sure first place was his.

"Horning said to me as I went by, 'You've got it; it's all yours,'" remembered Allen. "I had no idea I was in first. I thought there were five or six other guys up there somewhere, and I didn't find out there wasn't until five miles later. I was really surprised. It made the whole thing a lot easier mentally."

Behind Allen, however, Molina and Tinley were coming up hard. He rolled into the transition area with his lead intact, but ran out only 30 seconds in front of Tinley, who had biked in third, then gained a good 30 seconds on Molina during the change. With all three men moving east along Carmel Valley Road, two questions were on everyone's mind: How long could Allen hold them off? And, could Tinley avoid being nailed by Molina during the final miles as he had in two shorter races earlier in the year? The answers were not long in coming.

To everyone's amazement, Allen's lead didn't shrink; it grew. By the five-mile mark, he had more than a minute. More importantly, he was beginning to believe in his own mind that perhaps he could win. In his first competitive half-marathon ever, could he really hold off the two best runners in the sport? Scott Molina sure didn't think so.

"Tinley and I were running *hard*," he said. "I kept thinking to myself, 'He's gonna die, he's gonna die!'"

But Mark Allen didn't die, even after he crossed the finish line. He did smile, though. And he looked a bit dazed at the thought of all the talent he had left in the Del Mar dust.

The racing for first place, however, was not over for the day, although many spectators and race officials with watches had good reason to believe it was. Leslie Mendez had begun her half-marathon 11 minutes before second-place Jenny Lamott had begun hers, and there was a 13-minute gap between the leader and Julie Leach. Sure 13 minutes is a long lead—anything can happen—but let's be serious.

Apparently, Leach was more serious than anyone. With a white cycling cap shading her eyes and a bright purple swimming suit under her black running shorts, the pretty 24-year-old from Newport Beach began making up ground with her first stride. By the 6-mile mark, she knew it was possible. By 9, at a loop in the course where competitors could see each other, she knew it was inevitable. By 10, the 13 minutes had shrunk to nothing, and Julie Leach was holding tight to first place.

"You've got to tell me if I'm pulling ahead," she called to her cyclist, but there was hardly a need for concern. Within a mile after passing Mendez, Leach had the road to herself, and within three she was the center of attention at the finish line, where she ran directly into the arms of her husband Bill. He had finished 30 minutes before, in seventh place among the men. The scene was simply further proof: triathlons have a way of resolving themselves in the most human terms.

THE IRONMAN/KAILUA-KONA, HAWAII

Swim 2.4 miles/Bike 112 miles/Run 26.2 Miles
October 6, 1982

In 1982, in an effort to make the Ironman Triathlon more accessible to athletes from parts of the U.S. where winter weather made endurance training difficult, race director Valerie Silk switched the date of the event from February to October.

Dave Scott at the October 1982 Ironman. He had the split in each event, a feat that may never be equaled. With his performance, he showed all of us that to be competitive in triathlons you had to train full time.

Predictably, the race—the *second* Ironman of 1982—was billed as a rematch between Dave Scott and myself, although there were several men capable of winning, including my brother Jeff, Scott Molina, Mark Allen, and Jody Durst, the first triathlete from the East Coast to break into the top ranks. The race was expected to be a real battle.

It wasn't. The October '82 Ironman was a landmark race because it showed the difference full-time training could make. Stung by his loss in February, Dave Scott had devoted his life to the sport. He'd quit his job, whittled his personal life to a sliver, and, as a result, climbed off the plane in Kona about as fit and as focused as a human being can be.

Scott's performance that October was phenomenal. He had the fastest splits in each of the three sports—a feat that may never be equaled. And he won the event by 20 minutes. Really, the only battle of the day among the men was for second place.

From the *San Diego Running News*:

> . . . Almost seven minutes faster than the top swimmer in February, Dave Scott sprinted up the ramp in first place, followed closely by 24-year-old Mark Allen, a dark horse who had raced well against Tinley and Molina earlier in the year. He'd never gone the full Ironman distance, but his appearance at Dave Scott's heels added tremendous credibility to his challenge.
>
> Scott was on the road first. Slower on the change, Allen followed, then caught Scott, and the pair raced the clock through the bleak lava fields toward the turnaround at Hawi, the northernmost town on the Big Island, some 50 miles away.
>
> Jeff Tinley, third in February, came out of the water eight minutes behind Scott and Allen. His brother Scott, the defending Ironman winner, was out two minutes later. In front of them were plenty of tough athletes and 138 long hot miles of riding and running. The chase for the Ironman trophy was on.
>
> At Hawi, Allen and Scott were still together, although the end of the race for first place was coming much sooner than anyone expected. Scott made a quick move at the turn, dashed down the hill, and picked up a quick minute on Allen, who worked hard to gain back the lost ground. Hard, that is, until his rear derailleur broke and left him standing, helpless, by the side of the road without a bike and without a chance. He'd gotten much closer to Dave Scott than anyone would all day.
>
> Scott, meanwhile, gleaming in his white skinsuit under the hot sun, intent on the road and mildly concerned over a tightness in his right hamstring, didn't even notice that his competition was gone until miles later. But his lead had grown in the space of a brief snap of alloyed metal from less than a minute to more than 10. And it continued to grow. He flew into the bike-to-run transition area at the Kona Surf Hotel 16 minutes ahead of Scott Tinley and Scott Molina, 18 minutes ahead of Jeff Tinley and Jody Durst of West Long Branch, New Jersey.
>
> All four of the men closest to Dave Scott were running up the big hill

leading away from the Kona Surf at the same time. All four of the men were excellent runners, and on almost any given day each could challenge Dave Scott in the marathon. But not on *this* day. Like so many of the athletes who would follow them back out onto the lava fields toward the turnaround at the airport, they had been beaten badly by the terrible headwinds at the north end of the cycling course. Already exhausted with 26 miles yet to run, none of the four were in any condition to look for the man in front. Instead, they were doomed to spend the next three hours worrying about the man behind, hoping at least to be able to hold on to the places they had paid such a heavy price for.

Clearly the day belonged to Dave Scott. His final run down Alii Drive was triumphant. No one had won an Ironman so impressively. With the growing sophistication of the top competitors, many had expected this edition to be a dogfight to the end. Instead, Scott had time to drink, enjoy the attention of the crowd and the press before a weary Scott Tinley crossed the finish line in 9:28:03, 20 minutes and 5 seconds off the winning time.

THE MALIBU TRIATHLON

Swim 1.5 miles/Bike 100K/Run 20K
October 30, 1982

At Ironman that year, a slickly produced red, white, and blue brochure was circulating, advertising a race to be held just three weeks later, on October 30: "Triathlon—United States Championship." While most athletes shrugged the title off as hyperbole (Championship of what? According to whom?), the centerfold of the leaflet caught everyone's attention. Right at the top of the page was the heading "Prize Structure," and below that was a listing of $14,300 worth of cash awards, including $2,500 for first—same for men and women—and $1,000 to the first over-40 finishers.

What became known as the Malibu Triathlon was an organizational nightmare, plagued by terrible weather, frigid water that decimated a top field, and a jurisdictional squabble between law enforcement agencies that left an already dangerous bike course largely unmonitored. But the Malibu Triathlon was important in that it was the first race to attract a group of "professional" triathletes with the lure of a substantial prize purse. And it brought the athletes to a race that featured significant distances less than a month after the Ironman, something only money at that point in time could have done.

Photographs of the Malibu race show very few happy faces, even among the top finishers. In the numbing, sub-60-degree water, men and women with long swimming backgrounds foundered, and the Zuma Beach lifeguards more than had their hands full trying to pull hypothermic athletes from the water. They got to the lucky ones, but the unfortunate majority were on their own. In my own case, and I'm sure in the case of many others, it was only fear and a certain blind determination that got me to the beach. Mark Allen almost didn't make it at all:

"When we started heading back toward the beach, my arms started feeling numb," he said. "I was trying to make my muscles do something they didn't want to do. The signals just weren't getting through. Then my mind started getting foggy. I started getting water in my mouth, and I had to roll over so that I could breathe air and not water. It was scary. I'd go for a while and then call for help, but there was no one around, so I just kept swimming. I'd never experienced cold like that before. I didn't know where I was."

Hypothermia took 19 out of 75 starters out of the race. A broken collarbone removed me—I blew a front tire on a steep downhill and went over the handlebars. The day belonged to the survivors; talent and technique and strategy were merely side issues. Ferdy Massimino, a physician from Benicia, California, who had been 10th at the Ironman, ran through a driving rain and finished first among the men in just under five hours. Julie Moss, bouncing back after a disappointing 14th place in Hawaii, won the women's race by more than seven minutes.

As frightening as that morning in Malibu was, it paved many roads leading toward the future. It forced everyone to realize how dangerous a triathlon could be—how responsive a race director must be to the competitors' safety. The ripples of *that* lesson spread far beyond the scope of the mere 75 starters. Certainly, the race forced the wet-suit issue. It wasn't long before wet suits were not only legal in triathlons, but actually mandatory in some events.

Malibu also pointed out that, assuming you were well trained, recovery after major triathlons need not be a matter of a month of two. If you could race frequently, and if there were going to be races with prize purses in the $14,000 range, was it not possible to become a professional triathlete? Added to the sobering experience of being run over in Hawaii by the full-time training machine Dave Scott had become, that realization struck particularly hard in my mind. The time had come to make some commitments.

THE NICE (FRANCE) TRIATHLON

Swim 3K/Bike 100K/Run 30K
September 10, 1983

When I was in New Zealand in the spring of 1982, competing in NBC television's "Survival of the Fittest" after my win at Ironman, I met Barry Frank, vice-president of Trans World International, the television production arm of the International Management Group.

Frank was fascinated by the sport of triathlon and expressed an interest in becoming involved. Specifically, he saw great possibilities in a European triathlon staged to rival the Ironman in Hawaii in location, depth of field, and television appeal. He asked for my opinion, and out of our discussions came the idea of a tricountry triathlon. The race would start in Monte Carlo, cycle into Italy, and run back into France.

In May 1982, as a consultant for IMG, I flew to Monte Carlo for meetings with the local sporting organizations. A course was set up that fulfilled most of the original concept, although the bike ride was condensed to a criterium course mostly within the borders of Monaco—on much the same route used by the Grand Prix de Monte Carlo. We were all set to go for late summer when Princess Grace died in August and a six-month moratorium on sporting events within Monaco went into effect.

In an attempt to make the best of the situation and something of all the groundwork that had been laid, IMG's London office staged the first Nice Triathlon on November 20, 1982. It was a haphazard affair, with only 55 entrants, and the water was almost as cold as it had been in Malibu, but it was a landmark, too. The race introduced the sport to the European continent and introduced American triathletes to an event staged by a major international promotional company for one simple reason: profit. IMG and NBC, the television network that purchased the broadcast rights, had made a significant investment. They were looking for an exciting, salable product. They were looking for good theatre. They found exactly that.

Mark Allen began a string of consecutive Nice victories in 1982, although the small size of the race that first year and the haste with which the package had been put together kept his win from being very highly considered within triathlon circles. His fame, and the drama that the television and promotional people were looking for, would come almost a year later, at the 1983 edition of the Nice Triathlon.

Year number two in Nice was better in an organizational sense, and there were six times as many athletes as there had been the year before. Unfortunately, gaping errors in logistics left a bad taste (sweetened considerably by the largest prize purse ever in a triathlon—$50,000) in the mouths of visiting Americans. One particular error made a very lasting impression on Mark Allen. The story appeared in the October 1983 issue of *The Running News*:

> . . . The Americans were heavy favorites. Some 200 Europeans were entered, but they didn't seem to be doing much training in the days prior to the race. At least not that anyone could see. The Americans waved to each other as they passed during early morning runs along the Promenade des Anglais; they got together for bike rides to preview the breathtaking bike course; they swam together in the Mediterranean before breakfast—and wondered collectively where all the competition was hiding. The fact is that most of the British and European athletes were taking a casual attitude toward the whole event, a point underscored at the big dinner on Thursday night before the race. The thing *started* at 9:00 P.M., and most of the Americans were beginning to yawn even before they walked in the door of the restaurant. Confronting them when they did were long tables set with bottles of wine and Cassis cocktails for everyone. Water was conspicuously absent.
>
> While the Americans sat uncomfortably beneath the persistent glare of television lights and cameras, the rest of the room partied with a vengeance. The first course was thinly sliced heavily salted pork, the second a French meat-filled pasta in a heavy cream sauce, although by the time *that* was served, the Americans had gobbled what bread they could find and gone back to their hotels to sleep, having had more than enough of the noise and confusion.
>
> The party went on without them, of course—a postmeal cabaret kept most of the other jolly competitors bounding in their seats for hours. Isn't triathloning bloody fun?
>
> Well, no, not really. *After* the racing is over, perhaps, but there were quite a few unfunny faces on the beach on Saturday morning at 9:00 A.M. The

previous day had been overcast and humid, but the clouds were gone on race day, and all the triathletes standing at the water's edge at the Opera Plage knew they were in for a long, hot afternoon.

At the sound of the gun, half the field was off quickly, working hard for the first buoy. Dave Scott, Molina, and Allen led the way. At the rear of the field, some 50 or 60 novices entered more cautiously, minding the pebbles on the beach, entering the water gradually, then gently breaststroking their way onto the 1.8-mile course. Long afternoon, indeed.

Through most of the swim, Scott Molina was in front, with Allen on his toes, drafting. Then, just before the last buoy, Molina broke away, swam hard to the shore, and climbed the steps to street level with a 10-second margin. Allen was second, and a British swimmer, Mick Flaherty, was third. Dave Scott came next, right next to the first woman, Jann Girard. Up the steps they went, and the excitement in the transition area began to build. Allen changed first and was off, then Molina pedaled away, followed by Dave Scott. Scott Tinley, wrapped in skintight red, white, and blue, was four minutes back; his brother Jeff, sputtering angrily over getting lost in the swim, was even farther behind. The race was on.

For race officials in Nice, the bicycle course was a source of both pride and frustration. Scenic and challenging to a degree never seen in the U.S., the route was the main cause of the Americans' excitement about the race after its debut in 1982. One hundred kilometers long, it was composed of a long out-and-back section topped by two mountainous, heavily wooded loops.

Prerace literature indicated that the shorter loop, the one to the east side of the River Var, would be done last; the longer and more scenic loop, which wound through the Gorges des Vesubie, up through the towns of Levins and Aspremont, high on the west side of the river, would be ridden first. But when Mark Allen flashed through the traffic circle at the loop intersection and headed for the bridge, he was shouted down, then turned around, and pointed in the direction of the shorter loop.

Coming hard on Allen's heels, Molina saw Allen backtrack and adjusted quickly—he was suddenly in the lead as the climbing began, although both men were shaking their heads at the confusion. Why the sudden change of plans?

In fact, there had been no change. A mistake had been made. No race official had been on hand to tell the *gendarmes* where to send the riders. The bottom line was that all the competitors would have to do the course backwards and try to fight off the ill feeling of heading off in a direction they knew was incorrect.

Allen caught Molina along the flat stretch of highway leading to the town of Plan du Var and the beginning of the second loop. The pair rode together through the magnificent gorge, flanked on both sides by towering granite walls covered with moss, low shrubbery, and, higher up, tall pines. The river bubbled to their right until they crossed it at St. Jean, where they took a sharp right-hand turn up the hill and pushed on toward Levins. For miles there was nothing but climbing, switchback after switchback, through several small towns that seemed too picture-postcard-perfect to be real.

The reality of the race itself, on the other hand—the difficulty and the intensity of the climbing—was never in doubt. Nor was there any doubt that a serious logistical problem was beginning to develop.

By the time the first 20 riders had gone through Aspremont, at the top of the climb, several complaints had been heard that water was hard to come by at the aid stations. Unschooled volunteers were either standing by helplessly or handing the competitors water bottles full of an unfamiliar electrolyte replacement that seemed to be doing more harm than good.

Feeling the heat, knowing that it would only get worse, many of the Americans were becoming genuinely concerned, afraid they'd be beyond help when the going got really tough on the run.

On the long, flat stretch of road leading back into Nice, the lack of water was only part of what was beginning to bother Scott Molina. Mostly, he was very tired. Next to him, Mark Allen was still hammering relentlessly away, trying to build on the big lead over Dave Scott and Scott Tinley. Would the man never stop? Finally, three miles from the finish line, Molina backed off the pace, hoping to recover a bit before the run.

Allen, however, kept on, flying back into the transition area at the Opera Plage, changing quickly, then running back the way he'd come. He was 3 minutes ahead of a burned-out Scott Molina, 9 in front of Dave Scott, and 11 in front of Scott Tinley, who had missed a turn on the bike course near Aspremont and lost some time. At the four-mile mark, tired and slightly discouraged, Tinley assessed his own chances of catching the men in front of him with bitter brevity: "Ain't got nothin' left."

Few of the men in the top 10 did. "Looks like Mark Allen's day," shouted a television commentator to a passing press vehicle. And it certainly seemed as if the curtain had come down for good at the 1983 Nice Triathlon: Mark Allen's day.

In fact, the final scene was yet to be played. The curtain would come up again in Nice, raised by the tragic lack of water on the flat, hot, almost desolate run course that stood in stark contrast to the cool, shaded hills north of the city. "God, it was hot out there," Dave Scott said later. "There wasn't nearly enough water. It was *atrocious*!"

It was sad, too. Allen had a 10-minute lead on Scott by the 10-mile mark on the run, but he was getting tired. Flanked by a large escort of motorcycles and bicycles, he was maintaining the pace. His long, lean, muscular legs were still striding a steady cadence, but they weren't going to be able to do so for much longer. A worried look was in the leader's eyes, and he asked the question more than once: "How far back is he?"

By the 18-mile mark in the run—with 2 miles left to go—Allen's legs were rubbery, his face pale, and his eyes were frightening black pinpoints of desperation. He was still running, but only barely, and when a cyclist handed him a bottle of water that he sorely needed, it was too much: running and drinking at the same time was more than his body was capable of. His legs buckled, and he went down, breaking his fall with his hands before his knees actually hit the red brick of the promenade. He stood up slowly, confused and surprised at the position he found himself in. Could he move? He took one tentative step, then another. A few steps later, to the cheers of the crowd that began to move with him, he ran.

Not once during the final mile did Allen's vacant eyes shift from the narrow corridor of concentration that led to the finish line. He seemed unaware of the crush of spectators around him, screaming support in French, or the motorcycles pressing close with cameras probing. Afraid of falling again, he began to walk, briskly, swinging his arms high at his sides. He ran again only when he was sure he could finish the final 10 yards and up the low ramp that marked the finish line and the end of his ordeal. Then he literally fell down the other side into the arms of a friend. Dave Scott finished four minutes later, totally unaware of the drama that had preceded him.

"I just couldn't believe I had to walk," said Allen later. "Molina's talked about it. I've *seen* people have to walk, but I never thought that I would experience it. In Panama City [an earlier race where Dave Scott had caught Allen late in the run], I felt really bad, but I didn't have to walk, and I felt about as bad as I thought I could ever feel and still finish a race. But you know . . ." Allen stopped and shook his head and laughed. Jeff Tinley, sitting nearby, laughed too and completed the thought: "Boy were *you* wrong!"

The accuracy of the statement put a big smile on Allen's face. "Boy," he repeated, "was *I* wrong!"

IRONMAN 1983

Swim 2.4 miles/Bike 112 miles/Run 26.2 miles
October 6, 1983

It had been a big year for the sport. The growing sophistication of the competitors and the equipment they were using put a greater and greater emphasis on tactics and racing ability. Mere survival was no longer enough. At the Ironman in '83, the race between Dave Scott and myself emphasized that point as perhaps no race before or since has done.

Dave and I had traded wins in '82, so the potential matchup attracted plenty of attention, with good reason, as it turned out, because the other guys expected to challenge—Molina, Allen, and John Howard—all had problems of one kind or another and were never factors.

I came out of the water that year seven minutes behind Dave. I caught Molina around mile 40, and he looked just *awful*—he was barely moving. We were both on Team J David at the time and had been training together all year. As I went by, he glanced over at me with a drawn look on his face, and he said, "You know, you could win this race." I just kept going. As it turned out, his back was hurting him badly, and he eventually dropped out.

I caught Mark Allen just before we started climbing up the hills toward Hawi, and he was *really* surprised to see me that early. We rode together for a while, until the course marshalls started to give us a hard time. Mark dropped back a little bit then, and I took off and just opened the gap. It was really windy that

year—gusts up to 50 miles an hour—but I had a heck of a good bike ride anyway. When I dropped Mark, I knew things were going well, so it didn't surprise me when I started to get reports that I was gaining a lot of ground on Dave.

I finally caught him just before the steep hill about four miles from the bike-to-run transition area at the Kona Surf Hotel. I remember going by him, but I also remember feeling bad at that point—I'd pushed the bike hard. Still, I was excited to be finally in the lead, so I finished the course without doing anything to prepare for the run. I didn't stretch, didn't relax, didn't change pace, didn't take any fluids. It wasn't until I'd changed and headed out that it struck me how badly I felt. I was dizzy, dehydrated, and my legs were concrete. Halfway up the hill leading away from the hotel, I walked. All I could hope at that point was that my legs would come back to me.

It wasn't long on the run back into town along Alii Drive before I heard the helicopter overhead and then the pat-pat of a pair of shoes behind me. Sure enough, it was Dave, and he went by me looking as fresh as a daisy.

My biggest mistake was not going with him, not pushing myself hard enough at that point. I was too lost in my own fatigue to realize that he'd put on a big surge as he went by, that he'd gathered himself together to look as good as he could so that I *wouldn't* chase him, so that he'd demoralize me. And his plan worked, because the farther away he got, the more I thought within myself that the race was gone.

At the turnaround point at the airport—the 16-mile mark—Dave had a three-minute lead. We'd passed each other when he was on the way back, and I remember thinking that there was no way. I still felt terrible, even to the point of having to stop occasionally and walk. How would I make up three minutes?

I was desperately trying to talk myself out of winning. I began hearing reports that Dave was looking worse than I, but they were hard to believe when I'd just seen him and he looked so good. Of course, he'd just put on another show, but it was a lot easier to accept what I'd seen for myself as the reality.

Three miles later, the gap was well under three minutes; then under two minutes by the 20-mile mark. More reports came that Dave looked—and I remember this phrase particularly—"*real bad.*" People kept telling me that I had a chance, but I was still very serious about *not* having one. It was like being on the borderline of having to go totally beyond myself or stay within and make sure I didn't spend the night in the hospital. I was ready to have to work that hard.

At mile 23, Dave was only a minute and a half ahead, and I knew there was something wrong with him. I started to pick up the pace, testing, just to see. To my surprise, I loosened up; going to that next level had gotten some of the kinks out, so I continued, feeling better, really, than I had during the entire run. It wasn't until I crossed the finish line that I learned how close it really was—just 33 seconds—and how bad Dave Scott had felt during those last 5 miles.

Hindsight is easy, of course. There were a thousand things I could have done to make up that tiny gap during the long, hot nine-hour day. What I remember most of all was that I had sold myself short; I had given up on myself several times. Surely, that was lesson number one. But lesson number two had broader implications: the difference between Dave and me worked out to a quarter of a second per mile over 140 miles. Our finish made it obvious to all that triathlons of any distance could be *raced*, not merely survived, and that the difference between first and second place might be as little as a poorly tied shoelace.

TEAM J DAVID—TRIATHLON'S BRIEF ENCOUNTER WITH LIFE IN THE FAST LANE

It was every triathlete's dream. It was the reality of a select few. Some of us had been picked because of our success in the sport, others for their friendship with the right people. All of us were taken in by the grandeur and the affluence. Money seemed to be no object, and our futures—as athletes, as members of the financial community, as *anything*—looked bright. It was a triathlon fairy tale too good to be true, yet we lived it anyway, hoping that it would last forever.

It didn't even come close. The dream ended badly and abruptly, the celebrated Team J David revealed as just one expensive plaything among many of a company whose only assets were greed and a desire for high living, and whose only product was disappointment.

The collapse of the paper empire of Jerry Dominelli in 1984 rocked the San Diego financial community, but it didn't surprise the few who had been skeptics all along—stockbrokers and traders who watched the previously unsuccessful Dominelli gather around him a core of "experts" who knew nothing. The public story was that Dominelli was making huge profits trading wisely in the international currency exchange. In the end, though, his supposed wizardry was nothing more than a naked piece of classic fraud, foisted on people who wanted badly to believe the unbelieveable.

Mark Allen, Scott Molina, Julie Leach.

No one wanted to believe more than the members of the J David triathlon team. The good life had been ours: weeks and months of training in San Diego punctuated by periods of ridiculous opulence in places like Maui and Nice, France. But who was complaining. Not me, although I considered myself more skeptical than the others. Not Mark Allen, nor Scott Molina nor John Howard. Not Kathleen McCartney or Julie Leach. We were the cream of the international triathlon crop and the apple of the J David eye. The company spend a half a million dollars (an informed, but conservative estimate) on us in 1983. But it was all other people's money—part of it, in fact, was mine and Howard's and Allen's. We got sucked in like everyone else.

The team began in a very small way in mid-1981, when Dominelli agreed to help a pretty young co-ed from Newport Beach, California, named Kathleen McCartney train for the February 1982 Ironman. Among other things, he bought her a bike. The other members of the "team" were several J David investors who also happened to be triathletes.

McCartney won the race, and triathlon fever within the company began to grow. By the February 1982 Ironman, the team was more organized and the trip to Hawaii was a genuine group function. Kathleen had designed a distinctive rainbow team logo, there were new uniforms for all 11 members, and the style of living was J David all the way: they brought along a pair of bike mechanics, a swim coach, a team photographer, a video crew, and a masseuse. Still, it was by no means an elite group by triathlon standards. The chosen few were investors and special friends of the company. The attachment was more social than anything.

The moving force behind the team was 39-year-old Ted Pulaski, the top J David salesman and the man who had brought McCartney to the attention of Dominelli the year before. It was largely as a result of Pulaski's enthusiasm that his company became an Ironman sponsor. One thousand competitors in the October 1982 race found the fruits of the last-minute $15,000 effort in their race bags: a set of white shorts and a running singlet with the J David logo screened tastefully in small letters over the right breast.

The change in the team structure began around the time of the first Nice Triathlon in November 1982. Nancy Hoover's son George (Nancy was Dominelli's partner in the J David firm) had become heavily involved in the sport, and his mother was encouraged to support athletes who were his close friends. At the same time, Pulaski, more enthusiastic than ever, had begun to lean toward pulling the best in the sport together under the company banner. By the first of the year, the core group of stars had joined the team and were being paid a monthly stipend. We began to train together, and in March 1983, we took our first team trip—to Maui. It was the only time we all flew first class at company expense, but the trip set the theme for the year and fueled the rumor mills for a decade. The golden egg of the triathlon world had been laid and we were it. They called us "Team Bitchin'."

The training base for 1983 was Pulaski's sumptuous hacienda in Rancho Santa Fe, California, a fabulously affluent settlement north of San Diego. Members of the team would meet there—Tuesday was the day we'd often *all* meet—and run and bike through the hills and sometimes swim in his two-lane lap pool. Despite the bitterness about the outcome of the J David affair, none of us would ever deny that the group workouts were a big help. We pushed each other hard, and traded little tricks back and forth all the time. There was an incredible amount of camaraderie and expertise flying around that was totally unrelated to the money.

Little else, though, was unrelated to money. I don't think that any member of the team will ever forget the way the cash flew. At the Nice Triathlon in 1983 the team stayed at the famous Hotel Negresco along the Promenade des Anglais. I remember one day three limousines pulling up in front of the hotel and as I watched, the Hoover/Dominelli party came tumbling out: an assorted group of friends and family, the pilot of the company jet they'd flow to France. For a triathlon? It was bizarre.

"When I was sitting in the hotel room at Nice," remembered Mark Allen, "I was looking around thinking that it was all something out of F. Scott Fitzgerald. 'Is this Mark Allen?' I asked myself. 'I can't believe this!' "

We all shared Mark's incredulity. Nancy and Jerry were extravagant, but Ted was worse. His zest for spending was unbounded, and it was at his urging that we rented an entire complex of villas at the Mauna Kea Resort, 40 miles out of Kailua-Kona, when the team flew to Hawaii for the 1983 Ironman. For the first five days I was by myself in a house that could have passed for a palace. At a daily rate of $500, it might have *been* one, too.

The team took a little public relations heat for where we stayed in Hawaii that year. We were remote, physically aloof from the other triathletes in the race. Some of the complaining was sour grapes—our training sessions from the day the team started had been populated by athletes hoping to catch the eye of Pulaski for possible recruitment—but looking back, a lot of it was fair, too. We *were* remote. Overwhelmed at what the year brought us, we hadn't stopped to think of how that looked. No one else caught in the J David storm had stopped to think, either. I guess that's why the whole scheme worked in the first place.

Dominelli had been with us at the Ironman in 1983 and had been impressed, In November, team operations expanded. We were given space in the opulent J David offices in La Jolla. With Kathleen McCartney and me as co-captains, and in part spurned by some of the criticism we'd received in Hawaii, we started to develop projets that might raise the team's profile and eventually make it self-supporting. A national clinic series was discussed, and I started to think for the first time about a book project and a line of clothing. But the dream was about to end, the fantasy was about to become a nightmare.

In late January, 1984, Don Bauder, financial editor of the *San Diego Union*, broke a story about J David checks to clients bouncing. There had been some frightened looks around the office before the article, and a rumor here and there about some trouble, but soon there was panic, then collapse. The company had been at the crest of the mountain, glamorous and mysterious. Now the slide to the bottom of the mountain began, and it carried with it some of San Diego's most important people.

By late February, the bankruptcy trustees had taken over and the company offices were strictly off-limits to anyone but officials of the court. I found that out quite innocently by waltzing up the back stairs one day and trying to unlock the door to the team office. My key didn't work. Before I could leave I was approached by a marshall.

"What are you doing?" he asked angrily.

"Trying to get into my office," I replied, as if that wasn't obvious.

"It's off-limits," he said.

So I left, and that was it. Everything had been impounded: team equipment, personal effects, even trophies we had won at races.

But the team and its activities and budget were only side issues in the multi-million-dollar scam. That point was underscored in November 1984 when a huge public auction as held at the La Jolla Village Inn to recoup some of the swindled investors' money and help pay the mounting legal fees of the bankruptcy proceedings. Two thousand spectators had been expected, five thousand showed, jamming the big circus tent and overflowing into the parking lot where nine Dominelli sports cars sat as feature attractions. The top bid of the day was $116,000 for a bright red 1956 Mercedes Gullwing convertible. Two hours before that bid had been made, the J David triathlon team had been represented publicly for the last time—by a box of "Ironman jogging shirts." In the catalogue the box was listed as lot number M (for miscellaneous) –37. The winning bid was $150.

13
ONWARD AND UPWARD

I entered this sport by chance, because it was something different, because it looked like fun. When it stops being fun, I'll quit, cold. I'm serious.

I suppose that means having fun is my primary motivation for doing triathlons. It's more complicated than that, of course; I race to win, because when I win my wife and I eat, but I can't imagine training six, eight hours a day and having it be a day-in, day-out drudge. No, I'm definitely enjoying myself, and I expect that I'll continue to do so long after the day passes when winning is even a remote possibility.

The best and worst parts about any activity are the people, and triathlon is no different. They're all part of the education: the promoters and race directors whose sole interest is profit; the organizers who profit by doing the best they can do for the competitors. I'd like to think that in the long run that second variety are those who win out. As active triathletes, we have it in our power to make sure they do.

My greatest reward in this business has been the self-realization and self-confidence I've gathered in the face of a lot of self-doubt and perspiration. Are you confronted with yourself and all your fears at any time more clearly than when the pain of competition forces you to look? If at the 18-mile mark in the marathon at the Ironman Triathlon, with the temperature on the lava fields well over 100, you have doubts as to who you are and what the hell you're doing . . . well, you learn fast or quit. The figures indicate that most people learn.

The sport will certainly continue to grow and become more organized and complex, and that in turn will keep the crusty old pioneers like Tom Warren shaking their heads and wondering where the basic values—the insanity, the

THE FUTURE CHAMPS

I was trying to be as inconspicuous as I could be, standing off in a corner wearing a hat, sunglasses, and a newly-shaved upper lip. Not that anyone was going to recognize me—not at the "Whittier (California) YMCA Kids Triathlon"—but I didn't want to give even the most remote impression of being a "Little League Parent." I was in Whittier to watch my 13-year-old brother, Ted, compete in his second triathlon. It was his day and his show.

To my surprise, though, I *was* recognized. "Hey, ST, you trying to sign up for a kids' race?" came a high-pitched, pre-pubescent voice from below. I looked down and recognized 13-year-old Daniel Schwartz, the son of a San Diego-based sports photographer I knew, who was also entered in the race. "You must be awfully hard up for a win!"

I scowled at the little rat and threatened to pull the "ST" tri-shorts I'd given him up over his ears. He headed off to get his skinny little arms marked.

Few of the kids at the Whittier race, my brother included, had trained more than casually. That was as it should be. Triathlons can be tremendous fun for kids; the move from event to event is tailor-made for them, but the distances should be short enough to allow for spontaneous participation. They were in Whittier: a 1-mile run, 6-mile bike, 125-yard swim in the YMCA pool. Competitors ranged in age from nine to 14.

Few of the kids had any idea of how to pace themselves for the mile run, so there was a rush for the lead right from the start. Ted was up near the front. So was a kid who had decided that running with his bicycle helmet might save him some time in the transition. That might not have been a bad idea except that the helmet was huge—it looked like something Darth Vader might wear to a cocktail party. Maybe the kid had played some football and was used to it.

By the end of the bike, Ted as in first, probably doing a heck of a lot better than I would have at his age. He was followed by the kid with the wild helmet.

The bike ride had been composed of two three-mile loops, a feature great for the spectators, but potentially hazardous for the kids. Cycling is dangerous under the best of circumstances. In large groups, with the steadiest riders at the mercy of the least steady, the odds for harm increase dramatically. While the situation in Whittier was handled well, a single loop or an out-and-back six mile course with no hills, few turns or traffic intersections would have been better.

Ted dove into his assigned age-group lane of the five-lane, 25-yard pool with a big lead. And despite the fact that his big brother was pushing a line of triathlon clothing, he went in wearing knee-length plaid walking shorts. They were all the rage at school, I guess, but they acted as sea anchors for Ted. There was some momentary concern among the Tinley clan that one or two hot age-group swimmers—finally in their element—might catch him, but his lead was more than enough. He was a winner, a hero. He even signed some autographs for some of the younger competitors after the race.

For me, the race was a refreshing look at the way triathlons can be when the only real goal is friendly competition. The kids cheered for each other even during the race, worked hard themselves, and ended the day laughing, regardless of where they had finished. Maybe there's a future for kids' triathlons in this country. Restricted to short distances and held on interesting, safe courses, perhaps incorporating cross-country-type running to further reduce the potential for injury, the events would serve to introduce the sport to youngsters gently, before they are thrown into an adult race where the competitive atmosphere is intense.

Some Tips for Putting on a Kid's Triathlon

Keep It Short. For ages 9–11, maximum distances should be a 150-yard swim, a five-mile bike, and a 1–1½-mile run. For ages 11–14, try a 200-yard swim, a 7-mile ride, and a 1½–2 mile run.

Keep the Course Simple. Round-trip or out-and-back courses are best. No one gets lost and you can spend more time making sure everything is okay and less time directing traffic.

Keep It Safe. A course set within the confines of a park or in a location where roads can be completely closed is almost mandatory when it comes to kids on bikes. The short swims call for pools, not large, open bodies of water. Require hard-shell helmets and institute and enforce bike safety inspections.

Keep the Parents Out of the Transition Area. First of all, triathlon is an individual sport and should be presented as such. Second of all, the kids should be the ones racing, not the parents. Third, crowded transition areas are dangerous.

Emphasize the Fun. Be generous with your awards and dwell on the "everyone is a winner" concept.

spontaneity, the sense of challenge—have gone. The answer, of course, will be that it hasn't gone anywhere. Hundreds of thousands of first-time triathletes—each a pioneer in his or her own mind—will enter the sport in years to come, and for each the challenge will still be fresh and real; the TRIATHLON will still loom large in their minds, at least as large as it has ever loomed for anyone.

For all of its complexity, the triathlon will always be a very basic sport. It takes the kid in all of us—the one who ran his butt off playing tag or challenged her friends to bike ride up the hill or dared himself to swim out to the float at camp for the very first time—and turns him or her back into a real person.

At the staring line we all move back to square one: bank presidents, doctors, and entrepreneurs become what they used to be before they were bank presidents, doctors, and entrepreneurs. The first one to the raft wins, although just getting to the raft—even if you're last—is a whole hell of a lot better than being stuck on shore, too afraid to try.

The triathlon is life on the physical edge, so the impressions it leaves us are always keen. I never stop wondering at man's ability to move freely in an element as foreign as the sea— swimming in a triathlon has given me moments of both great exhilaration and great fear, but it has never been dull. And the thrill of flying down a long, smooth hill on a well-tuned bicycle at 40 miles an hour has always been, for me, well worth the climb back up the other side.

As for running, my favorite, it never fails to give me back the effort I put into it, no matter that I'm moving fast through New York's Central Park or slowly through the lava fields of Hawaii's Kona coast. There will be balance in my life as long as I can run.

I hope you've enjoyed the book. I hope it helps.

See you on the road.

INDEX